KRISHNA
BUS TOUR

KRISHNA BUS TOUR

Mitra Das

ISBN 9798877210202

Contact the author:
mitradasa@gmail.com

Book design:
Eight Eyes, eighteyes.com

CHAPTER 1

Krishna Road

I found Maharha sleeping on the couch. "You were moving around so much last night," she said. "You kept me awake."

"Sorry about that."

"You have a lot going on." She folded her bedding, because the living room should look nice even if it's at four in the morning. "Whoever buys this house is lucky. You did a good job on it."

"It only took me twenty years." I helped her carry her blankets upstairs. "Now I've got two weeks to finish the soffit and fascia, some paint in the kitchen ..."

"Is that what you were doing in your sleep? Climbing ladders? It seemed like you were dancing."

"I might have—"

She opened the closet. "This house is a work of art."

With the bedding put away, it was time for our morning meditation rituals. The two of us sat in the temple room I'd sketched out on graph paper many years earlier. A peaceful morning of focus would ensure a productive day. The birds hadn't yet started their morning song, there were no distractions, but my beads tangled into knots as I counted prayers on them. I had to pull them out of their bag several times to untangle them. I tried to bring my focus back to the mantra.

I was determined to prove the astrologers wrong when they'd said we'd be moving soon. We loved our location, the house, and the land.

Another interesting thing the astrologers said was that Maharha and I would enter a happy period, "Like when you first met, only better."

Maharha glanced with concern as I pulled my beads from the bag yet again to disentangle them.

The previous day, young men in rusty pickup trucks had bought my tools, while their wives in long, home-made dresses picked over Maharha's kitchen things.

We'd been just like them when we'd moved to North Carolina—twenty years younger and buying broken tools at yard sales. Now it was our turn to pass things along.

As the sky reddened, I went outside to chant with the birds.

༼༚༼༚༼༚

Ours was the first family to settle on the dusty dirt road surrounded by three hundred acres of Krishna community. The county said we could name the road if we picked something they could pronounce. We called it Krishna Road.

Our community grew. Krishna Road was busy, especially in the summer, when families drove to the pond at one end of it, their kids hanging out the car windows calling our son, Narayan, to join them. Each day, Chitra would gallop by on her white horse at teenage speed, followed by Lalita on her four-wheeler.

From our dining room window we'd watch the kids from across the valley walk down the hill and disappear into the treeline along the creek, to emerge again in the field where vegetables grew in straight rows. We'd try to guess who they were.

"Is that Tilak?"

"I think it's Vish."

"Who's he with?"

If my work was done, I'd join them at the pond or take a few kids up the creek in our backyard to play on boulders and in waterfalls.

All those kids eventually grew up, went to college, and moved away. And then there was no more traffic on Krishna Road and a for-sale sign on our driveway.

࿐࿐࿐࿐࿐

My son helped load the car.

"We're not coming back," I said. "After the tour you're going straight to college. Are you going to miss this place?"

Narayan pushed his duffel bag into the trunk. "Not really."

Maharha carried large grocery bags out from our house. "This bag is your lunch and this one is snacks, and this one is ..."

"Thanks, Mom," Narayan said.

"Make sure you eat this first. I put spoons in this bag and—"

"I wish you could come with us," I said to Maharha. "I know they'd love you on the bus tour."

"I would enjoy being with them." Maharha said, "But I need a little time to myself."

"You'll have plenty while we're gone," I said.

The three of us hugged, still not used to our son being taller than us.

Krishna-Road gravel crunched under our tires as we drove past the empty houses.

"Here we go again," I said. "Five hundred miles to Alachua."

"Plenty of snacks." Narayan patted the bags.

"We're well stocked."

This wasn't our first bus tour. Over Christmas break Narayan and I had ridden deep into Mexico. This summer was the twentieth anniversary of the bus tour program, and the tour organizer said this one would be the "mother of all bus tours," your chance to scratch everything off your bucket list—Niagara Falls, Yosemite, the Grand Canyon—with fifty of the best people in the world.

"I just noticed something," I said to my son, "you're the same age as the bus tour."

"Oh yeah, twenty!"

"Any news from your phone? You've been on it all morning."

"A lot of kids are coming from England."

"Anyone we know?"

"Not yet."

"There were a couple of British kids with us in Mexico. What did you think of them?"

"They were fun. Not what I was expecting."

"What were you expecting?"

"Mmm, boring."

"And polite?"

"Yeah, but they were fun."

"And they speak our language!"

Narayan returned to texting friends, leaving me alone with my thoughts. I was determined not to worry, but it was like trying to keep my tongue from probing the space where a tooth had once been. Moving is on the list of the top five events that cause stress, and here I was, driving merrily across the country, leaving my wife behind in a house for sale and our things packed in boxes. Also, I'd been dropped from my job just a week before the tour. I suddenly found myself unemployed, which is also on the top five list. Maharha was dealing well with the changes. When the news came that I was unemployed, she urged me to keep my word, saying, "They're counting on you; they need you to drive the bus."

We didn't even know where we were moving to. We'd become restless, like birds about to migrate. Maybe zigzagging across the country would give us a clue where to land.

It wouldn't make us any money, but it would be fun. Was I being selfish?

"Dad?" Narayan was exploring the snack bags. "How are you doing? Do you want me to drive for a while?"

"Sure. We'll stop for gas pretty soon. I can use a break."

CHAPTER 2

Alachuanians

Our headlights cast eerie shadows through the Spanish moss hanging from the trees along the dirt road "Like the beginning of a scary movie," I said.

Narayan's face glowed in the light of his phone screen. "It's always dark when we get here."

The Alachua Krishna community had started out as a quiet farm project. Many of our neighbors from Krishna Road had been drawn here, attracted by the schools and youth programs. The bus tour was based here, staffed by Alachuanians.

"There they are." Narayan pointed to a row of buses across a field.

With no moon or streetlights, the light of a dozen flashlights bounced like fireflies around the bus. Narayan jumped out of the car and ran to a circle of young people in the shadows that hugged and shouted. These were the people he'd been texting all day.

They were glad to see me, though subdued in their reception of me compared to how they had greeted my son. I asked where Manorama was.

"He was over there," a girl's voice said, "but then he was over there. He's kinda like everywhere."

I found Manorama working on an electrical problem with the bus. He looked happy and tired. "I'm glad you're here," he smiled. "We can't do the tour without our drivers."

"Aww, I do it because it's fun," I said. "Where should I put my stuff? And how can I help?"

Manorama adjusted the flashlight strapped to his head and took me to another bus, a school bus with bunks and divider walls made of unpainted plywood. It was rough compared to the silver bus he had been working on.

"This is the boys' bus. You can take this bunk for now."

This would be my home for the next six weeks. Darkness hid my disappointment. The silver bus looked much better.

"Thank you. Is there anything I can help with right now?"

"Try to get some sleep. We're driving to Houston tonight."

I saluted, "Yes sir!"

Manorama smiled and went back to his electrical problem.

𝇉𝇉𝇉𝇉𝇉𝇉

As I slept on my assigned bunk, young men fluttered

about in the dark like cheerful bats. One of them sat on me. "Oh, sorry. We'll go outside."

ロロロロロ

A gentle voice woke me, "Mitra Prabhu, it's your turn to drive."

I forced my eyes open. The road noise was much louder when I pulled out my earplugs. "Where are we?"

"I don't know."

It was dark, and I didn't know who I was talking to. "OK," I said. "I'll be ready in ten minutes."

"I'll tell the driver."

The stranger left me alone. My watch said 2:20 A.M. I climbed from my bunk and braced myself as the bus turned sharply.

The driver was from England. "I'm really tired," he said. He didn't say the R in "tired." "Have you driven this bus before?" He dropped another R.

"No, I'll need a lesson." I tried to sound American so he wouldn't think I was making fun of him.

After locating the high beams, wipers, and horn, I was driving. It was like a sports car compared to the big silver tour bus we'd driven through Mexico the previous winter. The roar of the tires and wind whooshing under the door made it seem like we were going much faster than 63 mph, our top speed. I had traded peace and quiet to drive a noisy bus through Louisiana at 2:30 in the morning, the taillights of the silver bus my only scenery.

Houston was our destination; there we would attend the biggest ever North American Hare Krishna Youth Conference.

CHAPTER 3

Houston

"There's not a trace of nutrition in this." Kaliyaphani's sixty-five-year-old lips curled as he pointed to his plate of noodles. He was the driver who had introduced me to the bus the previous night. "I need a proper meal."

He pronounced it "pro-pah" in propah British fashion.

He scowled at the noodles as if they were sawdust. "I can't eat this."

A hundred young people fueled by these very same noodles ran about, setting up chairs and tables in the Gauranga Hall. One of them slowed to offer us another serving.

"Uh, no thank you," I said.

I turned to Kaliyaphani, "What *is* a proper meal then?"

"You know very well—rice … beans … you know …"
He waved his hands to help me understand. "Food!"

I had a feeling he wouldn't last long on the tour. We
needed him, though. There was a lot of driving ahead.

"I'll ask around," I said, getting up from my chair,
"… see if I can find something *propah*."

We were in the meeting hall of the Houston Krishna
temple complex—a great big room with a high ceiling
and a stage at one end. It could seat a thousand people.
"I'll go check in the temple."

The Houston Krishna community had just completed
their new temple structure. Every room was filled with
construction dust and the sparkle of newness. The temple
was clean and smelled of fresh teakwood imported from
India, carved into fancy doors and altars for the deities.

Devotees in a small dining area for temple residents
were happy to learn I was hungry. "Do you remember
me?" one of the girls asked.

"Of course. But I can't remember where I know you
from."

"Monterrey."

"Oh, yeah! That had been our first stop on the Mexico bus tour. I remember someone made tamales for all
of us …"

"Yes! That was my mom."

"Your mom? They were *so good*! Is she here?"

"No, she's still in Mexico."

"Well, please tell her that that was the best meal we
had in all of Mexico."

"Really?"

"Yes! Everyone who was on that tour still talks about those tamales."

My Mexican connection loaded plates and bowls for me. "I need something for a friend," I said. "He really needs chapatis, but he's too hungry to walk. Are there any chapatis?"

"I'll go check." She ran into the back room and returned with a small stack. "Sorry, this is all I could find." She helped me load two plates with steaming hot rice, beans, vegetables, salad, and the chapati.

On my way out the door I said, "Don't forget to tell your mom."

"Yes, definitely. I'll call her right now." She waved her phone.

"Adiós, haribol!"

൜൜൜൜൜

The British kids arrived from the Houston airport. For one brief moment they appeared timid and out of place, carrying their luggage into the Gauranga Hall, until the Texans and Alachuanians welcomed them with hugs and shouts. Chairs and plates of noodles were brought out, and things got loud again.

I learned that the youngest in the group was seventeen and the others were not much older. Radha Vinode had the biggest Afro I'd seen in forty years. "I'm glad they're back in fashion," I said.

"Oh, why thank you," he said in polite British. "I don't know if they're coming back ..."

"Well, they should," I said "and you're setting the

trend. I'm going to start growing one right now, right this instant." I pointed to my thinning hair.

Radha Vinode's eyes opened wide, then he laughed. "That was good! *So good*!"

᪥᪥᪥᪥᪥᪥

In his late twenties, Gopinath is one of the organizers of the event. He checked the microphone and ad-libbed before rows of empty chairs, pacing like a professor.

"We've chosen this name for our group, The Sanga Initiative. It was a conscious choice, this new name. I'll explain how it came about …"

Nonessential talkers were hushed as everyone found their seats.

"The first word is *The*. It's a definite article, used to specify a particular noun as opposed to the ambiguous *A* Sanga Initiative. It means this *specific* Sanga Initiative. We have an intention, a purpose, we exist as a unique entity. The next word, *Sanga*, means association—our company, the people and things we allow into our life, things that shape who we become. *Initiative* means we're intentional about this; we've made a conscious choice to bring good things into our lives. We're taking initiative."

The crowd cheered, 150 of them, young women and men growing gentle beards—students, graduates, some already working in the real world—this was their group. They wanted to be here.

Ratish took the microphone next. He's a big guy with a soft face. I'd seen him at previous Sanga Initiatives as a younger spectator.

"Go Ra*teesh*!" one of the boys shouted.

A couple more joined in, "Yeah *Rateesh*!!"

Suddenly, forty voices were chanting, "Ratish! Ratish! *Rateesh*!"

Ratish raised a hand to signal, "All right, guys, let's get on with this." The crowd broke into sustained applause, cheering as a smile stretched across Ratish's face. He spoke over the applause, "A couple of announcements need to be made ..." The clapping stilled as he assigned teams.

Next he introduced Kalakantha. "Many of you know him from last year's Sanga Initiative. He joined the Hare Krishna movement in 1972 at the age of 18. He currently manages one of the most successful and innovative Hare Krishna youth organizations, the Krishna House, at the University of Florida in Gainesville. He's conversant with issues young people face. He's written several books. "Let's give him a warm welcome."

There was a more dignified round of applause for Kalakantha, who was three times older than his audience.

"Thank you, Ratish," Kalakantha said. A few minutes into his talk he said, "Until we reach the age of twenty-six or so, our brains do not entirely coalesce. We're unsure who we are ..."

Twenty minutes later he concluded, "For your next exercise, you'll break into small groups and share confidential information. If you don't care to have deep, meaningful relationships, don't worry about keeping confidences. If you're satisfied with a shallow life, with only casual friends, by all means tell everyone what's been said." He scanned the audience. "But if you want to make the best use of these five days ..."

Narayan was in the middle of the group, taller than everyone else, I felt sorry for whoever had to sit behind him and try to see the stage.

ௐௐௐௐௐௐ

Manorama had arranged a room for Kaliyaphani and me. I've had a daily routine of pushups and yoga since 1983. "When I miss a day, I feel it," I said between squats.

Kaliyaphani positioned two chairs: "Makeshift parallel bars," he said. He'd pushed himself into a handstand over the chairs then eased his legs down to a floating frog position without trembling at all.

I looked up from my pushups. "How did you do that? You must do this a lot."

"Yes." He leveled his legs before him and did several dips with his thin, muscular frame.

"You don't do anything halfway, do you?"

"No, I don't," he said.

"I remember that drama you performed in North Carolina. It must have been ten years ago. You played the part for every character."

He smiled while moving into his next position over the chairs. "You remember that one, eh?"

"I could tell you've studied drama. It shows."

I opened my laptop.

"What are you—" his breath was strained, "—working on?"

"Just a couple weeks of ago I lost my job. I hope you don't mind sharing a room with an unemployed person."

"Pity."

At the Gauranga Hall, each team was given thirty minutes to organize a drama. One by one they took their turns onstage.

Radha Vinode looked at home on the stage. He didn't need a microphone—his Afro appeared to amplify his voice. *"Let's have a massive round of applause for the next event ..."*

Narayan's team made last-minute arrangements behind the curtain while he held the audience with some jokes. "What's red and really bad for your teeth?"

The audience shouted suggestions as Narayan peeked behind the curtain, "Now?"

We heard a loud whisper, "Five more minutes."

"Really? Five?" Narayan returned to his audience. "OK, what were we on? What's the riddle?"

"What's red and bad for your teeth," one of the girls shouted.

"Oh, yeah. A brick." He paused to let them finish laughing, "So, would you like to hear an inappropriate joke? Is there time? Would any of you like to be offended?"

They most certainly would, but there was another loud whisper from behind the curtain,

Narayan looked back, "You're ready?" then returned to his audience.

"All right, then. Thanks everyone."

Applause followed as he stepped off the stage and the curtain parted.

ᘓᘓᘓᘓᘓᘓ

A tall couple walked through the temple garden.

"I see you together a lot. Are you related?"

The boy looked annoyed. "You're the third person to ask us that. We're boyfriend and girlfriend."

"Oh, I see. It's just, you guys just look so comfortable together and you look like each other—you could pass for brother and sister."

"Yeah, we get that a lot," the girl said. They both had dark hair and big eyes. Palika had a British accent, and her boyfriend, Shyam, was from Florida.

I asked if they were part of the bus tour.

"Yeah, we're doing the whole thing," Shyam said.

"Did I see you with a ukulele this morning?"

"Yeah, Palika and I both play."

"Cool! We'll have the whole tour to work up some tunes."

Palika said, "I'd like that."

Shyam interrupted. "We're supposed to be helping in the kitchen right now. We'd better get going."

CHAPTER 4

The Professional

With the level of skill in this group, I wondered why they would hire outside entertainment. My generation would consider it a waste of money, but what do we know?

The professional entertainer played electro and trance dance music while announcing, "I'm just a guy in an orange jumpsuit, and you're wondering what the heck is going on, but today you get to play the *Go* game! The treasure hunt that's *not* a treasure hunt!"

The music rose to a crescendo. In his mock serious announcer voice he said, "You'll get to compete and win prizes to see which group is the best. Are ... You ... Ready?"

The crowd cheered.

The jumpsuit guy kept the music going. "On the floor

19

to my left are six lunch boxes. Each of the team leaders is to select one of them. Are … You … Ready?"

The crowd cheered.

"Choose well, Grasshopper. Your fate is in the lunch box. Ready … Set … *Go*!"

The music got even louder as the team leaders selected their Spiderman, Winnie the Pooh, or Dora the Explorer lunch box.

The volume of the music suddenly dropped. "Do you each have your lunch boxes?"

"Yes."

The music stopped for a dramatic silence.

"Have any of you opened your lunch box yet?"

"No."

"Good. Now"—he spoke in an exaggeratedly serious tone—"you … may … open … your … lunch box."

He then spoke quickly, like the disclaimer at the end of a commercial, "You will find a cellular phone device, similar to what you may already own. This device will give you instructions, which you are to follow. Document your progress with photos and videos taken with the device. When you take pictures or videos, I want you to hold the camera like this—like a hamburger, not a hot dog." He noticed the group making faces, protesting, "What? You don't like that?"

"We're vegetarians. We don't eat hamburgers or hot dogs."

"You're all vegetarians?" He looked incredulous. "How else can I say it then? How can I communicate this?"

Palika, in her proper British English, suggested, "You could say, hold it horizontally rather than vertically."

"Yes, very well then. Horizontally rather than vertically." He continued, "Your group will be judged for creativity and comedy. You're going to downtown Houston for further instructions. Readyyyyyyy, *go!*"

We filed out of the building and onto our two buses. With an extra hundred kids, we were three times our previous capacity. Hot Houston air blew through the bus's open windows as I followed the silver bus downtown.

Manorama and I sweated in our two buses, while the kids carried out their mission. A tiny fan on the dashboard kept me alive.

༺༼༽༺༼༽༺

It felt good to get the bus moving again, with sixty voices talking all at once. Walking into the air-conditioned Gauranga Hall felt even better.

Orange jumpsuit guy collected the devices and posted photos to a large screen, zooming in to faces in the group shots, "What is this guy thinking?"

The kids were immensely entertained, especially when he tried to read their names and the Sanskrit titles to their pictures.

After botching several he said, "Oh no. Guys, I'm not even going to try this one. Can I get a little help?"

"No!" they shouted. "No! We want to hear you say it."

"Really?"

"Yes!"

"Are you sure?"

"*Yes! Yes!*"

"OK, here goes ... Matajis at Kurukshetra."

Our sides were in pain, eyes wet from laughing at

everyone else laughing at the jumpsuit guy pretending to be puzzled when he showed a photo of Rama Das standing over a storm-drain grate, trying to hold his dhoti down in imitation of Marilyn Monroe.

CHAPTER 5

Texas Barbecue

I brought out my guitar, and Palika got her ukulele. Soon we had a Hare Krishna chorus of British girls singing harmonies.

The boys trickled in from their kitchen duties. Mali fetched his banjo from the bus. He'd brought it from England on his sister's recommendation that I might teach him. Mali was eighteen, living in the shadow of his famous parents and two older sisters.

"We were singing your sister's tune," one of the girls said.

"Yeah, I recognized it," Mali said. "From her latest recording."

"How does it feel to be in such a famous family?" I asked.

"I guess a lot is expected of me." He looked unsure of himself, and I felt sorry for him. It took me a full week to catch on that I had wasted a moment of pity on someone who was actually fine. He's got the same red hair as his sisters. He described his Halloween costume: "I tied several bags of bread to my clothes."

He let us figure it out. "Oh! A gingerbread man!"

⅋⅋⅋⅋⅋⅋

Lunch was noodles again.

I sat at a lively table as a young lady said, "I'm so excited! The bus will be in Toronto next week! I'll be able to invite all of you to my igloo."

"How will you fit all of us on your dog sled?" I asked.

"Some will have to use snowshoes then."

I had to lean close to hear over the other conversations going on in Gauranga Hall.

"My maple syrup is running low too," she continued. "You know, a lot of people really think we live like that. People have actually asked me if I have Inuit neighbors."

I turned to another young lady at our table. "What about you? What do you miss about Australia?"

"Oh, I'm still getting used to everything not being upside down … and I really miss riding my kangaroo. I understand we'll be riding horses in Arizona, but it's just not the same."

"Did you get to wrestle any alligators while we were in Florida?"

"Yes, a bit, but it's just not like back home."

I shouted across the table to the red-haired boy, "Mali, how are you getting by? Have you had your tea today?"

He smiled politely, and a girl interrupted, "On my first visit to America, someone offered me an 'English muffin.' I've never seen such a thing. I don't know why they call them English muffins."

"How do you see Americans?" I asked, "What are the stereotypes for us?"

"Fast food—"

"And super-sizing every meal."

A Texas girl said, "When I was in Italy, people were surprised that I was vegetarian, that I don't eat at McDonalds."

ഇഇഇഇഇ

The seminars were hard work. In them, the kids explored spiritual and emotional topics. Every moment was tightly packed. In the tiny spaces between sessions, someone sang Hare Krishna, accompanied by harmonium, with someone joining in on drum. Chairs were pushed

aside to make room for dancing. The organizers smiled, shrugged, and joined them.

A big kirtan was scheduled each day in the newly constructed temple room. The Texas-sized Krishna deity smiled from His altar and watched our kids dance.

My generation stood back, giving them room, witnessing the reincarnation of the Hare Krishna movement.

A hundred and fifty robes and saris twirled across the shiny marble floor. The future is in good hands.

The jumpsuit guy had complimented them, "You've got rhythm. I've seen you dance."

༄༅༅༅༅༅

They kept up the pace for five days. On the last evening there was a barbecue.

"We're in Texas," Ratish said. "You've got to expect that."

His team spent the day curdling milk and then soaking the curds in homemade barbecue sauce.

Tarps and cushions were spread around a bonfire at Radha Nila-Madhava Park. The sun went down and the kids lit tiki torches. Ratish wore swimming goggles at the grill, loading and turning shish kebabs. His assistants aimed flashlights at his work. Barbecuing is serious business for Texans.

Kids helped themselves to the barbecue and bottles of ginger ale. They took turns singing kirtans around the fire.

"Who wants another? We've got a bunch here—come get 'em." The boys at the grill had Hindu manners and talked like Texans.

Months of planning had gone into this moment: advertising, planning flights, seminars, and icebreakers. This is what the future of the Hare Krishna movement will look like.

"Who's ready for another?"

The Sanga Initiative ended on this warm, fuzzy scene of 150 friends in the glow of tiki torches and root beer. Our stomachs were full and warm from barbecued shish kebab curd, bell peppers, and eggplant.

CHAPTER 6

Eighteen Forever

The ignition key brought the orange school bus to life, its diesel engine shaking the keychain on the metal dashboard.

A boy held a clipboard and shouted, "*Roll call!*"

"One!" came a shout from the back of the bus.

Another called, "Two!"

Each of us had been assigned a number.

"Three!"

Kaliyaphani entered the time and odometer reading in his logbook then stepped outside to check the lights and tires.

"Where's twelve?" Someone was always missing at roll call.

Twelve was located. He apologized, and the roll call continued.

My number was eighteen. "I get to be eighteen again," I said to myself. No one heard me. "I've got forty years' experience being eighteen."

Kaliyaphani returned, wiping perspiration from his British brow. We studied the roadmap together—Toronto was our target, with stops in St. Louis and West Virginia.

Manorama's voice came from the walkie-talkie on the dashboard, "The girls' bus is ready. Do you have everyone?"

Kaliyaphani picked up the walkie-talkie and answered with efficiency, "Yes, Manorama, we've got everyone."

He pulled the lever to shut the door, released the air brake with a loud hiss, and we were on our way, exhausted but too hot to sleep.

"Every mile brings us closer to Canada," I said.

Kaliyaphani wiped his forehead and smiled.

༺༺༺༺༺༺

Despite driving all day, we were still in Texas.

Manorama's voice came over the walkie-talkie, "We'll stop at Walmart for dinner."

The Brits were curious. "We've heard about Walmart." They got their cameras ready and posed in front of the sign.

A blue plastic tarp was spread at the edge of the parking lot. Manorama's wife, Jaya Sri Radhe, supervised. "Get your bowls and plates and line up here …"

Dinner had been cooked in the back of the girls' bus at sixty-three miles per hour.

We ate burritos as Mano-rama pointed out stars and planets. "That's Venus and that's Saturn."

A girl asked, "How far away is Venus?"

"Well duhhh …" one boy said. "You can see it's right on the other side of the parking lot."

Nitya Lila appeared, pushing a shopping cart full of ice cream boxes. "Who's ready for ice cream?" she asked.

I cleaned my bowl and got into the ice cream line.

Nitya Lila was always serving. I'd never seen her sit and eat with the group. "I'll eat later," she'd say. "Let me serve."

꧁꧂꧁꧂꧁꧂

A sheriff's patrol car pulled up, "Everything all right here?"

There was a chorus of yeses, and the kids offered the sheriff some ice cream.

"Well, thank you," the sheriff smiled and tipped his cowboy hat, "but not today. Where y'all from?"

We took turns answering.

"England."

"India."

"Ireland."

"New York."

"North Carolina."

"Toronto."

"Welcome to Texas." The sheriff tapped the side of his car and smiled. "You see, we don't *all* ride horses. I hope you enjoy your time here. It looks like y'all gonna have a real nice summer."

They thanked him, and he moved on.

"He had quite the accent, didn't he?" a British girl said.

"Yes, I could barely understand him," said another.

ௐௐௐௐ

After dinner, Manorama huddled the group. "This is the first actual day of the bus tour. A lot of you don't know each other. Let's circle up, then each of you give your name, where you're from, and in one word or less what you'd like to get from the bus tour."

Twenty-five conversations began at once.

"One word or less?"

"Hey, I'm gonna try that."

"What do I want to get out of the bus tour?"

"In one word?"

"Or less?"

"Hey, listen up people." Manorama cupped his hands around his mouth, "It's not that hard. Make a circle, you know it's shaped like this?" He demonstrated with his fingers. "Remember that from school? OK … OK … now you're getting it … all right, who wants to go first?"

As the sheriff had predicted, they were having a real nice summer. A cast of fifty characters introduced themselves to one another.

Then Manorama said, "Let's make a double circle, one inside and one outside, so each of you is facing a partner. First, the inside person will say their name and three things they are into. I'll tell you when to switch, then the outside person will do the same. Then the outer circle will move clockwise to the next person. Everyone ready? Facing a partner? OK, *go*."

Twenty-five conversations started again. A young lady introduced herself to me. "I'm into yoga, gymnastics, and music."

"Oh, really? I hope we get time to do yoga with the whole group. We did that on the Mexico tour, on the beach."

"That sounds so fun. I hope we get to do that."

Manorama announced, "OK, now switch to the outer circle!"

"OK, my turn now," I said, "I'm into people, conversations, and circles. Hey! That's what we're doing now!"

"And you like driving the bus too, don't you?" she said.

"Oh, it's OK. I prefer standing in circles."

"And people and conversations."

"Hey, you're paying attention. We're getting to know each other."

Manorama cupped his hands around his mouth, "OK outer circle, move to the next person!"

The circle shifted. I stood before someone I'd been on five bus tours with already. He joked, "Hey! I already know you. You're from Idaho—you like herpetology and serendipity. Now you can say what you want about me. Tell me what I'm into. Say anything you want."

The session ended with everyone laughing and gasping for air under the Walmart lights as the bugs flitted around us.

ௐௐௐௐௐ

The bus engines started again, our signal to board.

"*Roll call*!"

The command echoed back down the bus. "Roll call!"

"*Roll call*!"

"Roll call!"

Finally someone said, "Oh, sorry ... One!"

Another boy called "Two" faintly, from way in the back. And so it continued until all twenty of us were accounted for. I was still number eighteen on the roll call. It felt good to be eighteen. I'd been eighteen all day and would remain so for the rest of the summer.

I radioed the girls' bus, "Everyone's here."

"OK, same here."

Kaliyaphani released the air brake with a *psshhhhhp*, and we were underway. Kaliyaphani said he could drive till midnight.

Hearos earplugs—all bus-tour drivers know how to work them: roll and pinch them as small as they'll go, then insert into your ears. Road sounds fade away as the material swells back to its original shape.

A cool breeze blew in and the bus rocked gently as the burrito and ice cream sedative kicked in.

CHAPTER 7

The Keeper-uppers

A light shone in my face. A gentle voice said, "It's your turn to drive."

I heard myself reply, "OK."

There was a rush of sound as I extracted the Hearos.

᠋ᓄᓄᓄᓄᓄᓄ

The only seat on the bus is the driver's seat. Twenty bunks and a bathroom fill the rest of the space. Everyone was asleep except the boy sitting next to me. "Can I get you anything?" he asked.

"No, thank you, I'm fine."

Bus tires roared over the pavement as a 63 mph wind whistled at our door. It was midnight.

The boy asked, "Where are we?"

35

"Arkansas," I said. "Does that mean anything to you? Arkansas?"

"Not particularly."

"I didn't expect it would. Have you ever been outside of England?"

"This is my first time."

Each of the boys had been assigned a half-hour shift to chat with the driver during overnight runs. The keeper-uppers are a bus-tour safety tradition. Chatting with the boys was my favorite part of the day.

I asked my keeper-upper, "What did you like best about Houston?"

"I really liked the *Go* game. Our team was really into the competition, and then, there was the barbecue. Everyone had grown so close by that last night. We'd been together only what, five days?"

"A lot of work went into creating that moment. The crew, they know what they're doing. They're definitely on their game."

"In England we have a similar group, but it's for new people—y'know, teaching them how to chant and stuff. Here, they were getting into deeper issues. I wasn't expecting that."

"So you have stuff like this in England?"

"Sort of. In England the groups are much bigger."

"But not the same."

"No, this was more specific—meant for us. I really appreciated it."

"Do you live near the Manor?"

"Yes. Most of us on this tour are from there. We grew up going to the Manor for festivals and stuff."

Bhaktivedanta Manor is the property George Harrison donated back in the seventies to be used as a Krishna temple.

"It was nice of George to donate that. What was it like growing up there?"

"I love the place. It's home for me; some of my earliest memories are there. It's beautiful—the cows, the old buildings, the gardens ..."

༺༺༺༺༺༺

It was easy to stay awake with so much to talk about—the conference they'd just come from, their lives back home, their plans for the future.

One boy wasn't as talkative. I asked what he liked about the Sanga Initiative. He became thoughtful for a long spell, then said, "Everything."

Another long silence followed as I gave him a chance to elaborate. But since that was all he seemed to want to say on it, I changed the subject.

"What do you do when you're at home?"

Again there was a long silence before he answered. "Study."

After another long silence, he asked me, "So ... uh ... have you done anything particularly interesting in your life?"

I didn't want to make him feel awkward by answering quickly, given his own long silences. I checked the rearview mirrors and instrument panel, then looked thoughtful before saying, "Not really."

This kept me wide awake, calculating how long to prolong the silence before asking, "How about you?"

He pondered the question for some time before asking, "Uh … what would you like to hear?"

Eventually he looked at his phone, "Oh, it's been a half hour. Guess I'll go wake the next guy."

"OK, thank you. Good night."

"Thank you," he said. "It was interesting."

ཉཉཉཉཉ

Narayan took his shift. "I want to move to England," he said. "I feel like my best friends are from there."

"That was fast. You just met these people."

"Yeah, I know. For some reason I really connect with them."

"They're really a presence on the bus tour this year. I feel like I'm in an 'arry Potter movie. We've got Hagrid and Hermione and …"

"I'm ready to move there."

"You know, it's always cold in England, gray and dreary …"

"But Dad … *friends*!"

I couldn't argue with that. A topic that had been discussed at the conference was, "What's your least favorite service?" That was followed by, "How can you make it your most favorite?" It was concluded that even the most menial chores are fun if you do them with friends.

"You've got a point," I said. "You've got your priorities right."

CHAPTER 8

Thank You

There was no escaping the heat. The air conditioner had been removed from our bus. "It never worked right," Manorama said, "and we were able to fit in one more bunk when we took it out."

I made a gallant effort to sleep, even when the sun crept around to my side of the bus and one of the boys sat on me with an "Oh, sorry."

"It's all right. You didn't know."

I tried to be polite, but my tone was frightening. Earplugs shut out the world as I pretended to sleep. I hadn't signed on to become a grouch.

I began to count my blessings each time I was awakened. Instead of cursing that my sleep had been disturbed, I took note of whatever little sleep I'd gotten and was grateful. "Thank You" were the first two words that came to mind whenever I woke up. I paid attention to the sleep I'd just gotten, like finding a ten dollar bill in my pocket.

The St. Louis Krishna community is not as large as Houston's; it's sort of an outpost. Fifty Krishna kids dropping in was the highlight of their year, so local devotees came to see the kids perform a drama and kirtan. Then, after a feast, our two buses headed off into the darkness— the ten-hour drive to New Vrindaban, the farm community in West Virginia.

"We want to get there for breakfast," Manorama said over the radio as I bunked down.

ကြကြကြကြကြကြ

Moundsville, West Virginia

"Anyone that's awake should get up here quick," I told my keeper-upper. "They'll want to see this."

I drove our bus over a narrow mountain road, past barns and tractors. A couple of sleepy boys came up front. "It's coming up pretty soon," I said.

"What is?"

"Just around one of these bends you'll get a glimpse. The devotees built it in the seventies. They call it the Palace of Gold. Tourists come here every day and—there it is!"

"Whoa!"

"Wow!"

I had to drive with both hands. Part of the road had fallen away a few years ago, and now there was always a chance that we'd suddenly find ourselves over what had once been the shoulder.

"The palace will reappear in a few minutes," I told the boys. "We'll be driving right by it."

"Devotees built that?"

"Yes."

"It's beautiful."

"And they had no idea what they were doing," I said. "They learned as they built it. OK, here it comes again. You get another look."

ﮩﮩﮩﮩﮩﮩ

Once we'd parked, the kids found the temple room as well as the harmonium, drums, and kartals and began kirtan. Some opted for small kirtans on the lawn overlooking the swan pond.

British kids posed with the peacocks.

"Did you see the palace on the way in?" I asked.

"No, but we heard about the palace."

"So this is your first time here?"

"Yes."

"It's a ten-minute walk up the hill. Do you want a quick tour?"

They agreed. A couple more joined and we headed to Prabhupada's Palace of Gold.

Walking quickly uphill, I spoke in broken sentences. "My wife helped to build this place ... way back, before I met her .... It was originally going to be a temple ... a Krishna temple .... That was Prabhupada's idea for this place—seven temples on seven hills ... like Vrindavan with the main seven temples."

We paused for stragglers.

"City folks," I quipped, "not used to hills. Prabhupada loved this place—the simple country life. He stayed in an old wooden building behind that hill over there, but devotees wanted to make him something nice. This building was for him to stay in. Gradually it got fancy. When he passed on, they turned it into a memorial for him. It's one of the biggest tourist attractions in this state. People come here from all over to learn about Prabhupada."

"The Manor in England is like that. We get tour groups."

"Yes." I said, "we're interesting people—good for tourism."

ꙥꙥꙥꙥꙥ

"We're coming up on the back, sort of like the back side of a peacock."

"Wow! This is quite impressive."

"Yes, but you can see the paint is fading and some bits are falling off there, but it's still impressive."

"This was built back in the early seventies," I said, "It's a challenge to keep it up. Look at those fountains. I've been here when all this was working, with fresh gold leaf and flowers everywhere."

"Wow! I can imagine. It's still really nice, though."

We stepped inside, where it was ten degrees cooler.

I let the building speak for itself, with its mosaic floor and walls, stained glass windows, crystal chandeliers, gold leaf, and carved woodwork.

"Wow!"

"Look at this marble work on the floor and the walls.

They were amateurs, but they made these intricate patterns. One of the devotees drove to North Carolina to get a load of granite. He selected the best pieces and drove it back here. He parked the truck on a hill and the load started to slide off. He was so absorbed in his work that he stood in front of it, trying to stop a load of granite with his hands. He got hurt pretty bad."

"He's lucky he didn't get killed."

"Yup. That's a dumb thing to do. But it gives you an idea what kind of foolhardy people would take on something like this. But in the end you have—"

"All this."

"Yes. They were really sincere, and they still are. I hope you get to meet some of them." I looked at my watch, "But we'd better get going. We're already late for lunch."

"Pity we couldn't stay longer."

"I'm glad we got to see this."

"Oh, one more thing," I said. "My wife painted a little section of the ceiling. Let me show you …"

"Like the Sistine Chapel?"

"Exactly, but much better."

⊓⊔⊓⊔⊓⊔

I found a minute to call home. "We saw your artwork at the palace."

"My artwork?"

"On the ceiling."

"Oh yeah. I didn't know what I was doing, but…"

"It looks beautiful."

"Something came in the mail today. It says you have to stay in the US to be eligible for unemployment."

"We'll be in Canada tonight, so that plan won't happen."

"We'll be all right," she said. "Don't worry."

"I haven't had time to."

"That's good. Worrying never helps."

"True," I said. "They're loading the bus—I have to go, but I want to let you know I have a plan. Do you want to hear it? I'll have to be quick."

"Of course."

"When I get back, we'll do kirtans at the college in Boone and talk with students. I'll ask friends if they'd like to support us with a hundred dollars. It's not a lot to ask, and we've got a lot of friends."

"You do."

"And I'm making more friends on this tour. We'll send them pictures of what we do, make them part of the team.

And if it's an annual thing—that they give a hundred every year…"

The bus horn tooted.

"I'd better run. I'm driving the first shift."

ꖴꖴꖴꖴꖴꖴ

The rows weren't neat or painless, but our ducks were finally lining up. I always wanted to be a full-time Hare Krishna, but a few things had to shake loose for that to happen, things like my job and my house.

Narayan won a scholarship at Appalachian State University in Boone, North Carolina. We'd join him for his first year. The college town would be a good place to start our new life.

I'd collected over a thousand email friends; people I'd met at hardware stores or national forests who'd shown interest in what we were about. These people get a note from me every couple of months with a little story or a lesson. They enjoyed my updates from Houston and asked for more stories from the road.

Maybe these people could keep our show going?

CHAPTER 9

Toronto, Eh?

Manorama didn't smile. "Get your passport and other papers ready before you go to sleep. We'll reach the Canadian border at one A.M. When they ask, tell them we'll be in Canada for a week. We won't be doing any work while there—we're on vacation. Don't say anything weird or funny or we'll be stuck at the border all night. If we look suspicious, they'll have us take everything off the bus and they'll search it."

We arrived at the Canadian border and waited at the red light until a uniformed official came on board. I reported that there were twenty of us, including the driver: ten from the US, ten from the UK, one from Ireland, and one from India. Our sleepy troop then walked into the office in their pajamas and full of suspense.

The desk people wore sidearms and were friendly but routine, "Thank you. Welcome to Canada. Next, please!"

With everyone back on the bus, one of the boys called out, "Roll call, eh?"

"One, eh?"

꙲꙲꙲꙲꙲꙲

Manorama radioed, "We'll stop at Niagara Falls, a quick little stop in the dark. Everyone run out, have a look, and run back in. Niagara Falls, one more thing to check off your bucket list."

I turned the inside lights on and the message was passed from bunk to bunk. We parked near the sidewalk. "Everyone up!" I said, "You get to see *Niagara Falls*!"

A groggy group stampeded by. "Do we need shoes?"

"No, it's pretty warm."

"I'm getting mine."

"You don't need them; let's just go."

The girls joined us, wearing pajamas with prints of ice cream cones and Disney characters. We heard the rush of water as we got closer, an ominous power in the dark.

The wind changed directions, blowing mist over us. The girls screamed and ran. The boys imitated them, screaming and running.

On our way back to the bus, the girls stepped in puddles with their stocking feet and screamed. The boys imitated again—this time Mali jumped into Radha Vinode's arms to be carried across a puddle. *These people are entertaining at two in the morning. No wonder Narayan wants to move to England.*

In Canada, the bus was no longer a toaster oven.

The Toronto Hare Krishna temple is an old stone church with pointed arches and towers. Devotees purchased the building in the 1970s, when the neighborhood was still affordable. BMWs, Mercedes, and Porsches lined the street near the temple. Occasionally a Bentley or a Rolls Royce cruised by. Hare Krishna bumper stickers decorated rusty Toyotas with prayer beads hanging from their rearview mirrors.

Two refrigerator trucks were parked in front of the temple. Volunteers ran up and down the ramps carrying trays and boxes, slamming the cooler door as refrigerator motors roared in the pristine neighborhood. Our economy cars blocked traffic to unload people and supplies as Ferraris waited politely.

The Toronto Hare Krishna devotees were preparing for their annual Ratha Yatra festival—a parade where participants pull a large, colorful chariot down Yonge Street, then the entire parade ferries across to Centre Island, where a free feast is served to anyone who wants to eat.

I figured the neighbors must be used to this, since it happens every year. Walking up the temple's stone steps, I wondered whether these neighbors ever visited the temple.

The shoe rack was overflowing, so I added my sandals to the pile on the floor. The lobby was a churning sea of smiles and hugs. Volunteers wore hair nets and carried trays of food through the crowd. But most of the people were in the temple room, dancing to a lively kirtan. I planned to shower and join them.

A kitchen volunteer helped me find the shower, then said, "There's a long line. Have you eaten yet? Everything is hot and fresh. Come, we'll take care of you."

"It's one of the rules of the road," I said, "to always eat when it's ready." That made him happy. I then took my place in the line, despite my friend insisting there was no need for me to wait. "This is another rule I follow."

He smiled, "Then with your permission, I should get back to my service."

"Yes. Thank you. You've helped me a lot."

He disappeared into the kitchen, which was filled with volunteers, cooking and singing.

I loaded my plate with authentic Indian cooking, then noticed Madhava waving, motioning to the empty seat beside him.

Madhava has a gentle South African accent. "Will you join me tonight with your guitar?" He asked, as if I'd be doing him a great favor. Every weekend he's flown around the world to sing at festivals. With Madhava, there's a guaranteed audience, ready to immerse themselves for hours in kirtan.

"Sure," I said. "What time?"

"Eight."

Muscles bulged from his sleeveless shirt; he wore an earring, like a pirate. Despite his appearance, there's nothing flamboyant in his speech.

"I really appreciate it," he said. "Your guitar—it adds a lot. And is your son here with his mandolin?"

"Yes."

"Can he join?"

"Yes."

"I really appreciate it."

༄༄༄༄༄༄

After breakfast, I congratulated the cooks, then began a search for a quiet space to chant on my beads. My next mission would be to find a quiet space where I could meditate for two hours, something I've done every day since December 1975. I have a string of a hundred and eight beads, and I recite the Hare Krishna mantra on each bead circling the rosary sixteen times.

Since quiet spaces are rare on bus tours, we have to make do with whatever space we can find. I would continue my forty-five-year habit no matter what came my way. I walked to the bus to chant, not stopping to look at anyone or the stone architecture or the landscaping or the interesting cars from the fifties or the kids walking in front of me singing cute songs or the signs written in both French and English. I didn't look at all this because I was chanting my japa.

When I arrived at the bus, the engine compartment on the back was open. Manorama waved me over. He looked concerned. "It needs to go to the shop."

"What's the problem?"

Dravinaksha pointed his flashlight at the radiator. "It's got a leak. It's pretty bad."

Manorama said, "It's a good thing we caught this now. In Toronto, we've got mechanics and a place for everyone to stay. It's a lot harder to deal with this on the road." Manorama was seeing the bright side and even showed a trace of a smile. "Can you drive with Dravinaksha? One of you will need to navigate."

"OK," I said, "I just had breakfast. I'm ready."

Dravinaksha navigated, calling out directions. "Turn left here. OK. Now we're on this for six kilometers …"

Dravinaksha and I have shared driving on several tours. This time he was on the girls' bus. I learned their air conditioning wasn't working well. "It gets really hot when they're cooking. But we're in Canada now. It's not an issue like it was in Texas."

Dravinaksha directed me to an ugly part of town full of potholes and broken buildings. I backed into a gravel lot full of trucks.

"It's a big job," the mechanic said as he wiped his hands on a rag. He was from India, and I saw even here he was servicing trucks decorated with Hindi and Punjabi scripts. "We'll have to take it out, clean it, and braze it. It'll take a full day to do it right."

"The temple recommended you," Dravinaksha told him. "They said you're the best."

"Hare Krishna," he smiled. "Bring it by tomorrow morning. We'll get right on it."

ௗௗௗௗௗௗ

The temple room was crowded. Narayan tuned his mandolin.

Madhava smiled at us, sat straight and tall before the harmonium, closed his eyes, and began. For one hour he sang the same melody, building slowly, etching the mantra into everyone's mind.

Hare Krishna Hare Krishna
Krishna Krishna Hare Hare

This is what everyone had come for—to taste the eternal. They could depend on Madhava to bring them there.

Narayan and I dressed the sound with our strings, like candy sprinkles, nothing distracting; we were there to support. Madhava's eyes were shut the entire time.

A drone hovered overhead, shining lights, aiming a camera as Madhava sang, "... *Hare Rama, Hare Rama, Rama Rama, Hare Hare* ..."

The drone flew to the ceiling of the old church, then back into our midst. Some pointed, but most found the kirtan more interesting than the distraction. Digging deeper and quickening the pace of his singing, Madhava said, "A little louder, from your heart."

When he introduced a second part of the melody, the kirtan soared past the drone. Many got up to dance. The lights were low, the sound was high, and it was a magic moment.

The magic lasted for two hours.

"One last time ..." Madhava requested again, "from your heart," then ended with Sanskrit prayers: "*harer nama harer nama eva kevalam* ..."[1] everyone reciting with him. Then "Sri Harinam Prabhu *ki jaya!*"[2]

The applause of two hundred people mixed with the

---

1 "The holy names of God are all you need to achieve your goal. Nothing else will get you there." *Brhan Naradiya Purana*

2 ki jaya, jubilant praise to Sri Harinam Prabhu, God who has appeared in the form of His holy name.

roaring in my ears. Madhava reached over and touched my knee, "Thank you." He folded his hands and repeated this with each of the musicians before the crowd fell on him, patting him on the back, thanking him. He was engulfed by hugs and praise. He stayed calm, letting the honors slide off. It's dangerous to let it go to your head. The magic only works if you're humble, when you know it's not yours.

CHAPTER 10

Centre Island

At the lakefront, a man in uniform welcomed the big silver bus with folded hands and a "Namaste."

Manorama folded his hands, returning the gesture. "Hare Krishna."

Manorama followed the uniformed official into his office and returned with a stack of papers. "They like us," he said. "We're bringing them a lot of business. Forty thousand people are coming to the festival, riding their ferry boat." He pointed. "And that's our boat over there."

"That little thing? For the bus?"

"Yup." Manorama put the bus in gear and rolled toward it.

"Is that ramp wide enough?"

He looked straight ahead. "We did it last year."

I looked for an open window and imagined swimming out of the bus. "I'm glad you're driving." I held my breath, the boat rocked then settled.

Manorama stacked the papers on the dashboard.

"What kind of paperwork is that? It looks like a lot."

"It's a release of responsibility." Manorama smiled. "If the bus goes overboard, it's not their fault."

"That's reassuring."

The little boat pulled away from the dock into open water. When we reached Centre Island, Manorama drove across another narrow ramp. He enjoyed maneuvering the oversized bus over the one-lane road, avoiding bicycles and joggers, until we reached our festival site. There he snuggled the bus between trees and festival tents.

The Festival of India crew greeted us, curious to see who was on board.

"Everyone's at the parade," I told them. "You'll see them in a couple of hours."

The Festival crew are volunteers who travel each summer, setting up stages and tents for Krishna festivals, the low-budget bus tour for young men.

Two hours later, passenger ferry boats brought loads of Krishna festival people to fill the tents and stage. Kitchen volunteers juggled pots and plates, moving people quickly through the line at the free feast booth.

Bus-tour kids dressed for the drama they'd been working on. Some dressed as demons, with black around their eyes and ugly costumes.

With two stages, there was constant tuning and rehearsing while the forty thousand guests watched the final product. Radha Vinode took the microphone, "Wasn't that wonderful?! Let's give them one more massive round of applause!" He then described our international group of Krishna youth traveling across North America in two buses as a cultural tour, performing music and dramas. "Put your hands together for our next act!"

I had an appointment with Madhava near a duck pond to work out the melody for the final kirtan of the day. He wanted it to be special. "How about this tune? Tell me what you think."

A couple of ten-year-olds found us and asked for Madhava's autograph. While signing their notebooks he asked about their lives and if they like to sing kirtans. "Next time I come to Toronto," he said, "I want to hear you lead a kirtan."

೧೧೧೧೧೧

A man was brought onstage for the final kirtan. "He played flute in the movie *Life of Pi*. He's really good. Give him a microphone!"

Madhava welcomed him. Everything was in place. Madhava began the invocation and the sound system broadcast peace across Centre Island. The flute replied tastefully.

The kirtan started slowly, like a heavy plane on a long runway. Once we were airborne, I saw tears in the flute player's red eyes, smelled alcohol on his breath, but decided not to notice. He was on our team.

Madhava kept the focus; he allowed the flute a solo, then brought us back to the mantra, reaching a dramatic pinnacle that surprised our drunken professional.

Offstage, the flute player congratulated each of the musicians, hugging and kissing everyone. The kids were curious—they'd never seen a drunk before.

௵௵௵௵

Our home, the orange bus, was in the shop on the mainland. We would stay overnight on Centre Island, the girls in their silver bus and the boys in tents.

That evening, Manorama called the boys together. "This is what gets the bus tour in trouble—boys wandering off with girls in the dark. This could shut down the whole bus tour. I can't be everywhere, and I don't want to always be the bad guy. If you see something, can I count on you to stop it?"

The boys pledged their support.

I was impressed.

There were no incidents, and Manorama was able to sleep.

௵௵௵௵

In the morning, our makeshift Krishna community had the entire island to ourselves. Sankarshan was running a booth at the festival, selling clothes from India. I spotted him walking toward the shower in only a towel. "You've sold everything in your shop except for this?"

Sankarshan laughed. "I wish. We did pretty good, but I still have plenty to wear."

"That would be fun, though, if you sold everything including the clothes you were wearing and went home dressed in leaves taped together."

"I would use dollars."

"That's a happy thought. I hope it happens today."

෴෴෴

Balancing on a ladder, Kaliyaphani touched up the paint on the silver bus. The lettering had been scraped going through a narrow toll booth in Mexico. "Anything will be an improvement," I said.

"Yes."

An hour later I gathered a few kids. "Look what Kaliyaphani's doing. Let's show him some love."

They applauded and took turns hugging him when he stepped back to look at his work, "You think it's all right?"

I said, "It's downright meticulous."

He beamed. He liked that word, meticulous.

෴෴෴

Sundari is the girl who'd joked about wrestling crocodiles and riding kangaroos in Australia. She performed graceful yoga poses whenever we were on solid ground. But she spent her day on Centre Island with a tall boy from the festival crew. They looked similar, with light brown, sun-bleached hair.

"Are you related?" I asked.

"No, we're boyfriend and girlfriend." Sundari's eyes flashed.

Here we go again, I thought.

"It's just, uh, well, you guys look so ... innocent together."

"We look innocent," Sundari replied in her Australian accent, "because we *are* innocent."

"Well, aren't you going to introduce me?"

"Yes, this is Haridas. He's from England."

Haridas extended his hand. "It's a pleasure to meet you."

"England is a long way from Australia—about as far away as you can get. Do you get to see each other very much?"

"No, not that often."

"Well, I don't want to interrupt. This is your precious time together."

"Oh no, that's fine," Haridas said. "After the summer, I'm moving to Australia."

"Good plan," I said. "If I was your age, I would easily go to the other side of the world if a girl like this was interested in me."

"Thank you."

"But how did you meet?"

"I met him in England last summer—the bus tour, you know?"

"Ah, another long-distance relationship from the bus tour. Let's see, we've got Sri Ram from Florida with Nayika from England, we've got Danishtha from Florida and Chandi from England, then we've got Shyam and Palika. Long distance used to be Canada and Florida, but now it's England and Australia. The bus tour is expanding."

"Yes, it is."

"Well, I'll be on my way. You two go ahead and keep your innocence."

"Of course," Sundari said. "You can count on it."

ꖚꖚꖚꖚꖚꖚ

It had been another festive day on Centre Island.

The weather was just right, people had been fed, entertained, and inspired, then ferried back to Toronto. The

Festival of India crew packed tents and stages into their truck with the help of the bus-tour kids. Girls in festive dress carried poles and tent stakes alongside the boys.

When the last tent canopy was packed away, it seemed time to relax, but Manorama announced, "Everyone on the bus! If we miss the last ferry we'll be stuck here overnight. Get on the bus right away!"

Two separate roll calls happened as the silver bus trundled down the narrow road along Centre Island. People made way for us and the girls hung out the windows, smiling, waving, and apologizing. Boats tooted their horns and their crews waved at the Krishna bus.

Waiting at the ferry dock, Krishna Prema turned to

Narayan to discuss some important matters: "I know some vegan jokes, but they're pretty cheesy."

Narayan, "Hey wait! Was that supposed to be—"

Krishna Prema, "Oh yeah, I mean, no, that wasn't intentional, but it works."

Narayan, "Let's try it out."

They tested the new joke on clusters of friends as Manorama drove the bus onto the last ferry to Toronto.

"We've got a new joke!" Krishna Prema pumped his fist.

"Note the time and place," I said, looking at my watch. "The birthplace of a new joke. The world will never be the same. They can erect another monument." I pointed to the bronze statue of Ned Hanlan, "the most renowned oarsman" in history. "What sort of statue should they make for a cheesy vegan joke?"

꒫꒫꒫꒫꒫꒫

When our ferry boat arrived at the mainland, Radha Vinode fell to his knees, "We made it! We're *free*! … free at last! Free at last!" Tourists—Chinese, tattooed, young, and old—walked around him as he bent down and kissed the ground. "We're alive! *Alive*! Look at the birds, the ground …"

When he saw the orange bus, Radha Vinode continued, "Home! We're home at last! *Oh*! There's no place like home! No place like home!"

"Get some sleep." Manorama told me. "We'll be at Serpent River tomorrow morning. Kaliyaphani's driving the first shift."

CHAPTER 11

Serpent River

"It's too bad we have to drive in the dark. This is one of the most beautiful areas in North America." Bhakti Marg Swami was my keeper-upper. He's walked across Canada four times! With his orange robes, one of the boys said he looks like a walking traffic cone.

"It's a bus tour tradition," I said. "We drive while everyone sleeps."

"Yes. Long drives are boring."

"Was this part of the route you walked?"

"Yes. It's hard to believe the main road across Canada is so quiet. People would sometimes join me and walk for a while."

When he's not walking, the swami oversees the

Canadian Krishna temples. "Management can make you shortsighted," he said. "Walking gives me a fresh perspective. My motto is, *Less squawking and more walking.* Impossible problems tend to sort themselves out."

"I've seen that happen," I said. "I've thrown myself at problems that wouldn't budge."

"But step aside for a moment," the swami waved his hand, "and let Krishna do His magic."

We rode in silence for a while.

"What can we do?" the swami said. "We're very small. We try our best, then Krishna does the rest. Speaking of rest…"

I thanked the swami for staying up with me.

Parikshit came up to take his turn. He's studying drama and wants to make a career of it. His trained voice is easy to hear over the road sounds. "I've never been around so many devotees my age," he said. "I grew up in Vrindavan, India. There are a lot of devotees there—nice devotees—but everyone is—" he glanced at me.

"Go on—go ahead and say it."

"It's mostly old people."

"Yeah, sorry about that. I apologize for being old."

"No, it's—I mean—*you're* OK, but sometimes old people can be discouraging."

"They forget what it's like to be young."

"Exactly! But with this group, we encourage each other. I feel I can do anything."

"Whereas with old people you feel stifled."

"Yes!"

"They can hold back your creativity; it's as if they're afraid of it."

"Absolutely." He spoke with perfect diction, I heard every syllable.

"I've got experience of that," I said. "You want to contribute, you've got ideas, but they hold you back."

"Really? You've been through that?"

For a brief moment I considered telling him why I was selling our house. "I don't want to forget what it's like to be young. When I joined the temple, everyone was young and full of ideas. We made plenty of mistakes—that's how you learn. People my age have forgotten what it was like. New ideas scare them."

Parikshit talked about his plans way beyond his allotted keeper-upper time.

"Oh no," I said, "I've made you break the rules. Sorry about that."

"No, I'm fine with it. Thank you."

"Get some sleep."

꠶꠶꠶꠶꠶

Narottam looked like a samurai with his long black hair and man bun. I asked him to turn his head toward me so I could hear him over the road sounds. He's from Alachua, studying at Santa Fe Community College. He helped get the Krishna lunch program going there.

"Is this a daily meal?"

"Yes. Every day."

"How many people usually come?"

"It's pretty small compared to Gainesville. We get about four hundred every day."

"Four hundred! That's a lot. And you're there every day to help out?"

"Pretty much every day. I help set it up, then make plates."

I shifted in my seat and glanced at the bus mirrors. The Trans-Canada highway was quiet at three in the morning. Everyone else on the bus was asleep.

"Where does all this get cooked?" I asked.

"At the temple. Then they drive it to the campus."

"You've outdone me, Narottam. You beat me real good. I thought I'd done something by setting up a couple of dinner programs at our local college. Ours was once a week. Fifty people would have been a big night. But yours happens every day."

Narottam smiled.

"You beat me, and I'm really glad. You did good Narottam."

Narottam looked at his phone, "Uh oh, it's four o'clock. I better get the next guy."

"Oh, yeah, sorry," I said. "I kept you up too long."

ꙮ

I found a lonely spot on the Serpent River where the river ran across a huge slab of stone. I crept barefoot like a tender-footed caveman and dipped in. The cold knocked the breath out of me.

Wide awake now, and drying on the warm rocks, I soaked up the sun on my back. It was a perfect spot for morning japa. I picked up my beads and was soon in the zone.

Someone tapped my shoulder. "There's a kirtan and class downstream. Will you join us?"

"Thank you," I said. I really meant it. I had my own

river at home and more solitude than I cared for. "Sure, I'll be right there."

Downstream, the girls had set the bus's Krishna altar on a flat boulder and decorated it with leaves and flowers. The others sang.

It was a rare bus-tour moment. Usually, we had to rush to be somewhere else or were part of a festival or onstage. Instead, it was just the fifty of us, sitting under a tree, singing songs by the river.

Manorama asked Bhakti Marg Swami if he'd like to speak a little. The swami looked surprised. "Are you sure? I don't want to interrupt."

The kids wanted to hear him. They insisted and moved closer so they could hear him over the river.

"Krishna ..." the swami began, "the Supreme Personali—"—and he made a motion of drinking tea with his pinkie extended.

"*Tea*!" a few kids shouted.

The swami continued, "... of God—"—then pointed to his head.

"*Head*!" a girl called out. The Americans knew the routine; the Brits caught on quickly.

"... was walking through the—"—the swami held up four fingers.

"*Four*!"

"... est," the swami said.

They laughed, oblivious to the world until pancakes and jam arrived.

Manorama announced, "Eat breakfast, go hiking and swimming, but be back at the bus by three."

Kaliyaphani set up a harness and ropes for tree climbing. "I'm a tree surgeon," he said. "I brought my equipment along."

"Really?" I said. "Cutting limbs up there?"

"Yes."

"Cutting trees on the ground isn't dangerous enough? Up there it's crazy dangerous!"

"Yes," he said, adjusting the harness around his waist, "very much so. We take precautions."

"I know you're in it for the money."

He smiled, "Mostly because it's a lot of fun."

"I can imagine."

With his harness secure, he pulled himself up the tree. He's built like a spider, thin and muscular. An audience formed, shouting encouragement and appreciation.

They each took a turn at climbing. He'd made it look easy. The kids respected his skills. "I want to be like Kaliyaphani when I'm his age."

"Kaliyaphani is the *man*!"

It started raining. "This will blow over in an hour," Manorama said. "We'll stay here for lunch."

Our bus was the only shelter. We had to close the windows to stop the rain from getting in. It got hot with all of us in there, and the windows fogged up.

The girls' bus was even hotter, since they were cooking in there. We saw the girls sticking their heads out into the rain for air and relief. Through foggy windows the boys watched a couple of girls dance arm in arm in the rain, splashing puddles and singing.

I climbed into my bunk and plugged in my Hearos.

When I woke, the sun was shining and the bus was empty. I grabbed my bowl and filled it with noodles.

Still wearing his tree-climbing gear, Kaliyaphani smiled and ate noodles.

The rain dancers stood together, giggling. Their dripping clothes made a puddle by the picnic bench.

CHAPTER 12

Thunder Bay

At two in the morning, Grappa took his keeper-upper shift. He has a Krishna name but prefers to use his last name, Grappa.

"It's such a cool name," I said. "I'd probably do the same."

The bus ahead of us signaled and stopped on the roadside.

"I wonder what's going on?"

Pranaya Keli came to our door. "We're changing drivers," she said. "It's going to be about fifteen minutes."

She glanced up at a pair of large feet hanging over the doorway.

"It's Narayan," I said. "It's the only bunk he can fit in."

"He sleeps like that every night?"

"Yes, he's used to it. We have to duck every time we go out the door." To Grappa I said, "This is Pranaya Keli. She used to be one of our neighbors in North Carolina. I knew her when she was this tall."

Pranaya Keli looked at my hand, "I've never been that small."

I raised my hand a few inches. "How about here?"

"Not quite."

"Hey, while we're stopped, there's something I've been wanting to see. I think you'll want to see it too."

"What is it?"

"The stars. We're a hundred miles from anything. I bet you've never seen it like this. Grappa, get your shoes." We ducked under the feet in the doorway and onto the roadside with Pranaya Keli. "We need to get away from the light to really see them."

"This looks beautiful!" Pranaya Keli said. "I've never seen the sky like this."

"Keep going," I said. "We need to get further back." We walked away from the taillights of the bus. "Wait till your eyes adjust to the dark. Right about—here. Now look at the horizon until you can make out the trees in the dark—can you see their outline?"

"Yes."

"OK, now look up."

"*Wow*!"

The sky exploded.

"That's the Milky Way—that band of white going across the sky."

"*Wow*! I've never seen it like this!"

"*Wow*! So many stars!"

"There's no moon tonight, no clouds, and no city lights for hundreds of miles. Perfect conditions."

"I'd heard of the Milky Way, but never seen it."

"So that's why they call it milky."

ᘓᘓᘓᘓᘓᘓ

"Radha Vinode, good morning!" I greeted him.

He yawned and chuckled. It was his turn to keep the driver awake.

"How's the tour going for you so far?"

"Quite well, thank you."

All day he's loud and dramatic, enunciating as if on-stage. At three in the morning I get to see his other side.

"I really enjoyed taking down the festival tents and packing everything into the truck. Did you know there's a slot in that truck for each pole?"

"Yes, I've loaded it many times. There are red slots for the red poles, green slots, yellow—maybe you'll get a chance to help set them up. It's like a giant Lego set."

"I'd love that! I love building things."

"It's something not many get to do anymore," I said. "I got to build the house I live in. We built several houses in our community."

"That would be my dream."

"It was fun." I didn't tell him we were selling that house.

Distant lightning flashes lit the prairie.

"Whoa! That one was awesome!" Radha Vinode said quietly.

"Like fireworks, great big fireworks. It looks like a heavy storm. Hopefully wc'll miss it."

I was dangerously sleepy when my shift ended and Kaliyaphani took over. The rain hit as he fastened his seatbelt. Kaliyaphani drove full speed through the heavy rain. He's a daring chap. Besides tree surgery, he races motorcycles.

"Uh, you'll need to slow down in this," I indicated over the roar of the rain. "You can't even see."

"Oh, shall we?" He looked up, turning his eyes away from the road. "Alright then." He lifted his foot off the accelerator, "There we go. How's that?"

"Go as slow as you need to," I had to shout, "but don't stop or we'll be rear-ended. Our best bet is to drive through the storm."

Kaliyaphani enjoys danger.

"Watch out at the bottom of hills," I shouted. "That's where you're likely to hydroplane. If you feel the back end of the bus slide to one side, you know what to do, don't you?"

"Yes, you compensate by steering in that direction."

"OK, sounds like you've got it. Have fun! I'm going to sleep."

"Alright, pleasant dreams," he shouted back.

"I'll dream of sunny skies tomorrow."

"Got it," he said in his very British accent.

"Cheerio, old boy."

೧೧೧೧೧೧

There were shouts in the dark.

"Oh my god! Oh my god! *It's raining in here!*"

Another voice joined in, "I'm getting wet! Hare Krishna! There's a leak! *The roof is leaking!*"

Flashlights and curses added to the confusion.

"Oh Krishna! *Oh Krishnaaa!*"

I was dry and off duty and let the boys sort things out. A bucket was located and placed under the leak. Most of the boys slept right through it.

CHAPTER 13

A Small Pond in a Big Fish

The park overlooked Thunder Bay. I joined the man on-stage who was checking the sound system. He was from the local TV station and dressed in a suit and tie. "It looks like the weather is going to be perfect today, yah know? We expect over eight thousand people. Every year it gets bigger."

"Wow!" I said. "Eight thousand people on a Tuesday?"

"You betcha! There's not much else going on in Thunder Bay."

"What's the population?" I asked.

"About eighty thousand."

"So ten percent of Thunder Bay will be in this park today?"

"Yes. And the other ninety percent will watch it on TV."

I rubbed my chin. "Maybe I'd better shave."

The park filled with people as Bhakti Marg Swami introduced the mayor and handed him the microphone. "Local government deals with weather, so we'll take credit for this beautiful day."

I applauded with the audience.

Next, a member of Parliament spoke and claimed that since the federal government handles weather, *they* should get the credit.

I cheered again.

Bhakti Marg Swami introduced each performance and entertained the audience between acts. Backstage he told our troupe, "Remember, you're on TV!"

Eighty thousand people in Thunder Bay saw the bus tour's drama and kirtan. All of this was brought about by a couple of Hare Krishna people who live there. They raised funds and organized the event, with free food and prizes for everyone.

꧁꧂

On the drive that night I told my keeper-upper, "Those devotees in Thunder Bay are big fish in a small pond. It's just one family, but they're making a real impact on that little town. We need more devotees like that. It's better to be a big fish in a small pond than vice versa. Because who would want to be a small pond in a big fish?"

CHAPTER 14

Winnipeg

Bus tour kids joked and laughed, chasing each other around the washing machines. The laundromat owner watched them carefully as he changed dollars and handed me the key to the bathroom.

"Hey, Dad." It was Narayan.

"Good morning, Narayan." Although it was one P.M., I'd only just woken up.

"Good morning, Dad."

"I'm heading over to the temple. It's at 108 Pleasant Street," I said.

"Wow! How did they get *that* address?"

"I don't know. It's almost as good as ours. But nothing can beat Krishna Road."

"We'll join you later."

ᖇᖇᖇᖇᖇᖇ

As I walked through town, I asked the locals where Pleasant Street was just so I could hear their Canadian accents.

"Oh, gosh, ya' know I think it's that way, eh?"

"OK, thank you."

"Yoo betcha!"

An ice cream truck drove slowly by, and kids jumped out of wading pools and ran to line up in their swimsuits and towels.

The two-story brick house at 108 Pleasant Street was

neatly landscaped. I knocked on the solid oak door, admiring the woodwork. A young couple greeted me, bowing their heads to the floor when they saw me.

"Wow! That's quite a reception."

"Welcome, Prabhu. It's so good to have you."

"How do you know? You don't even know me."

They smiled innocently. "Please let us know if we can get you anything or if there's anything we can do for you."

They escorted me to the dining room. The table was set with linen, elegant plates, and flowers in vases. Even the restroom had flowers in it, and neatly folded towels. Everything was in perfect order.

"This place looks like it's for sale," I said. "I mean that in a good way."

My hosts smiled.

I'd spent months preparing our house in North Carolina for selling. It would never look this pristine.

A woman at the dining table smiled and waved, silently apologizing as she and Bhakti Marg Swami were in a phone conference with another Canadian temple. I gathered she was the temple president.

Ms. President and the swami didn't mind if I listened in. The hosts quietly set a plate before me on the spotless tablecloth and poured me a tumbler of water. After a week of eating in parking lots, waiting in line for a glop of oatmeal from a stainless steel pot, I was glad to find myself sitting at a dining table with china plates and flower arrangements.

The voice on the phone described an overbearing person trying to take control. Bhakti Marg Swami calmly advised, "He'll be an asset for a while. Then people will catch on. He wants to help, so we should let him. When he becomes a problem, it will be apparent, and people will stop listening to him. He'll have to learn this lesson himself—we can't step in and fix everything."

It's easy to forget the scope of the swami's responsibilities. He's calm, but he gets a lot done.

I was still eating when the meeting ended. "I'm so sorry," Ms. President said. "I had to stay in the meeting."

"Oh, it's fine. It was entertaining to see you both in action, like watching a magic show or a basketball game."

The swami introduced me to Vrinda, the temple president, then excused himself and went upstairs.

"Did you get enough to eat?" Vrinda asked me. "There's plenty."

"I'm fine, thank you. This place is beautiful." I gestured to the vases on the windowsill and the lace curtains. "You've decorated tastefully."

"But it's a mess right now."

"I don't see a single thing out of place."

"No, it's a mess, I haven't had a chance to clean today."

"You and my wife would get along. She says that all the time."

We heard a knock on the door, and a tall guy my age walked in with a parrot on his shoulder. Everyone was glad to see him. The parrot didn't mind when the conversation grew loud and jovial. "He's used to crowds," the owner said.

A plate was set on the linen for him to share with his parrot. The rest of the group excused themselves. They had to prepare for the evening event. I asked parrot man his story.

He'd seen several temples come and go in Winnipeg, he said. He'd also assisted Bhakti Marg Swami on his cross-Canada walks, driving the support van and lining up speaking engagements.

"I'd go to radio and TV stations—people always listen to a guy with a parrot on his shoulder."

"That's something I haven't tried yet," I said.

꒰꒱꒰꒱꒰꒱꒰

Our venue that night was a beautiful old stone church. The sign out front announced a Bhakti Yoga Music and Dance Performance. The maintenance man gave me a tour with special Canadian words, "We had a _%_-ing leak up there." He pointed to the high ceiling. "You wouldn't believe how _#_-ing hot it is working up there …"

The night's show would take place in the chapel, which had a stage and a beautiful pipe organ.

I helped set up the reception room so the maintenance man could watch the show. We set up tables and put plates of samosas and cut fruit on them as well as flower

vases. We heard the final kirtan in the chapel followed by applause. "Here they come."

The maintenance man made his way through the crowd to tell me, "I've seen a lot of shows here. This was powerful. The guests really liked that song—they sang along and got all the words right. It was #___-ing special."

The bus kids packed up the sound system, costumes, and props and loaded them onto the bus while I made new friends. A conversation followed me out to the bus after everyone had snacked and packed; the bus engines were idling—giving notice that we were about to go.

The maintenance man appeared at my side, "I _*_-ing hope you guys come back next year."

"Yes!" I hugged him. "Keep the church in good shape for us."

With a full stomach, clean clothes, and cheeks tired from smiling, I was the last to board the bus.

␢␢␢␢␢␢␢

Mali joined me in the early morning hours, while I was driving. "Mali, good morning. How was your day yesterday? How did you like Winnipeg?"

"It was wonderful—my best day on the tour."

"Oh? Why's that?"

"Well, my mum used to live there. That's where she first met devotees."

"I wish I'd known. Should I turn around and go back?"

"Also, my grandfather is buried there."

"We should visit his grave—take a picture with all of us doing a kirtan there."

"All around, it was a great place. And the audience at the show—that was the best ever."

"We should get a small crew together and get a van and visit all these places at our own pace—stay as long as we want. What do you think?"

"I'd love it."

"We would need to bring someone responsible, someone like Nitya Lila. Have you noticed how she's always helping?"

"Yes, I've seen that."

"She won't eat until she's served everyone else. Did you notice that day when we stopped to dump the dirty water tank from the boys' bus? You guys were discussing whose turn it was when Nitya Lila came up with her rubber gloves, "OK guys, show me where it is.""

"Yes, I was awake for that one."

"Our mini bus tour would need someone like that, someone who thinks ahead."

"Someone to pour the milk on our cereal."

"Exactly."

CHAPTER 15

Naan Sense

Nothing happened in Regina, and everyone was glad. There was no national park, no river, no festival—just a chance for everyone to be in one room together.

The Regina Krishna temple was purchased in 1978—an abandoned church in a poor neighborhood. The foundation had settled, and every door and window was out of square. The kids loved it and sat on the sloping floors singing their kirtans.

Breakfast was served in the small backyard: naan, an Indian flat bread, served with sour cream, cheese, lettuce, jam, and peanut butter. Manorama incited a competition to make the best naan sandwich.

One boy said, "This is naan sense."

Another said, "I'm naan committal."

I joked, "Wait a minute. Is this naan vegetarian?"

We thanked our hosts for the naan traditional meal.

卍卍卍卍卍卍

When we arrived in Saskatoon, we parked the buses on a suburban street—a devotee family who lived on that street had given us the run of their house. The local Krishna kids then took the opportunity to throw frisbees with the bus tribe.

Ananda spent his day patching the roof of the bus. "I want to make sure it never leaks again." He's one of our first responders—always ready to help. We have a few of those on each bus to help things run smoothly.

I was about to join him when the boys brought a banjo and trombone out onto the lawn. We marveled at the soft grass, "It doesn't grow like this in North Carolina."

"Or Florida."

We serenaded Ananda until Manorama called everyone into the house.

"We'll be in Yellowstone National Park in a couple of days. We're going to take a group photo, and we want you all to wear one of these—" and he pulled a tee shirt from a box. Everyone approved with an "Ooooh!"

It was a silkscreen of Vishnu riding his eagle, Garuda. On the back, a bus with wings flew above the clouds.

"Each bus is named Garuda." Manorama said, "This is Garuda 1. He's been retired and is now in bus heaven. Under these clouds it says 20th Anniversary ISKCON Youth Bus Tour. This will be a collector's item, a piece of history."

Manorama's wife, Jaya Sri Radhe, handed out shirts. "You can wear them today, but keep them looking nice for the picture.

She tossed one to me.

"I get a shirt too? I'm just a driver."

Manorama raised his voice, "Listen up, everyone— tomorrow we'll be in Calgary. There's a Ratha Yatra festival."

CHAPTER 16

Calgary, Alberta

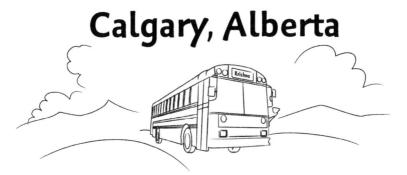

Narayan continued his last two weeks of college studies while on tour, then took his final exam at the Calgary Krishna temple on the busiest day of their year.

Volunteers cooked and packed and loaded trucks with supplies for the Ratha Yatra, while my son shut out the world around him and used the temple's wifi.

Our buses had already left for the festival site, and the temple was emptying fast. When Narayan was done, I asked around for a ride to the festival site. The only thing left was a delivery truck. "It won't be comfortable," our host said, "but I'll get you there."

We sat in the back of the truck on barrels of food bound for the festival.

"How did you do on your exam, Narayan?"

"I got an A."

"That was quick."

The driver pointed to Calgary's highlights, which we glimpsed through the truck's tiny window. "They've built tunnels up there so people can walk from building to building in the winter."

"How cold does it get in winter?"

"Minus forty, minus fifty. Life goes on; you do what you have to. It can get cold here even in summer. We're lucky to have such a nice day. There should be a good turnout at this festival."

꧁꧁꧁꧁꧁꧁

Another truck was parked in the loading zone, with devotees unloading supplies. "They've taken our parking spot," our driver said. He rolled his window down and called out, "Hare Krishna! How long will you be?"

The other driver answered by tipping his head from side to side. This can mean a lot of things depending on what part of India you're from. Usually it means everything's OK.

"Five minutes," he answered, flashing all ten fingers twice.

"OK." Our driver also tipped his head from side to side, but it was more abrupt, which meant he wasn't really OK with it, but he understood.

"He said five minutes with his voice, but twenty with his hands," I said.

"We'll be all right," our driver said. "Why don't you join the festival?"

"OK, thank you for the ride and the tour of Calgary." I tipped my head side to side to show how much Hindi I understand.

The park reminded me of downtown Delhi, tightly packed with people in saris and turbans. A long line stretched to the free feast booth, with people talking loudly and gesturing as our driver had.

The bus tour drama team had on their costumes. "We're on in twenty minutes." It looked like a challenging venue with so much activity.

The colorful, striped Festival of India tents defined the festival grounds. For us it was just another day on the bus tour, but for the locals it was a rare sunny day, a chance to meet neighbors and to connect with seekers who might be invited to visit the temple in the coldest part of winter. People walking by might think it was a family picnic for Indian people until they got called over to a booth for a free meal or a book.

༺༺༺༺༺༺

The weather held all day, and the sun stayed up late into the evening as local Calgary Krishna kids helped us pack up the tents.

A leader called, "Haribol! Grab a pole!" Then six people lifted the tent by its poles and carried it to the truck, where another team dismantled it.

The first group ran to get the next tent, "Haribol! Grab a pole!" while the next team stripped the tent down and packed it up before the next tent arrived.

The girls, wearing aprons and yellow work gloves, showed they could load the truck as fast as the boys, "Like packing our toys neatly away for next time."

With the tents packed away, there was an opportunity to tease each other. A tub of ice cream appeared, and the kids took turns riding a tiny bicycle. Important life skills for young adults.

CHAPTER 17

Yellowstone

"Tell everyone to get their passports ready." Manorama's voice came over the walkie talkie. "Entering the US is harder than getting into Canada. Tidy the bus so we don't look like a hippie caravan. If one person says something wrong, we could be detained for hours. We want to spend tomorrow in Yellowstone."

Stalwarts like Ananda relayed the message to the rest of the boys.

༄༅༅༅༅

I handed the customs border officer my passport, looking as wide awake as I could at one in the morning. The officer studied my face, then the passport. "Where are you from?"

"North Carolina."

"Are you here to get away from the sharks?"

There had been two shark bite incidents in North Carolina that summer. Manorama warned us not to joke with the officers. If they take it the wrong way, we'd be stuck all night. "Yes sir," I said. "I'm not taking any chances."

He smiled and handed me my passport, "Next!"

We took roll call on the Montana side of the border—and then were on our way to Yellowstone.

꧁꧂꧁꧂꧁꧂

Grappa was my keeper-upper. He's a muscular guy from England. Gentle and polite, he took every opportunity to do chin-ups on tree branches or the crossbars of Walmart shopping cart stalls. "That was an easy border crossing," he said. "They were pleasant."

"Yes," I said. "They asked if I was in Canada to avoid shark attacks."

"Oh, yes, I heard about that. But, you know, toasters are much more dangerous."

"I should have told him that."

"You're more likely to be electrocuted by a toaster than bitten by a shark. Every year a lot of people die from sticking things in toasters."

"I'll watch out for toasters from now on—give them a wide berth. Next time I see a shark, I'll tell it, 'If you were a toaster, I'd be scared of you.'"

"Yes, that should set him straight."

꧁꧂꧁꧂꧁꧂

Grappa was replaced by Shyam.

"Good morning, Shyam. Are you and Palika still getting along?"

"Oh yeah."

"When will we get together with the ukuleles?"

"Palika's been talking about it, but there's been no time."

"Manorama's working us too hard," I said. "Fast-paced bus life."

"There are a few more weeks of tour. It's gonna happen."

He's found a girl, been through college, and has a long life ahead of him. He carries himself with a calm maturity.

꿔꿔꿔꿔

"We're inside an active volcano," Manorama said. "If it decides to erupt, all of Wyoming and Montana will be destroyed."

Palika missed the first announcement. "What did he say?"

"We're inside an active volcano. There's a chance we could all die a loud, violent death today."

"Oh, lovely, a bit of suspense!"

"If we don't make it—I just want to let you know it's been nice having you on the bus tour, you and Shyam."

"Aww."

Manorama continued his announcements, "Boiling River is a short hike. That river you see down there is icy cold. A hot spring flows into it. Don't go into the pure stream of hot water! It's *way* too hot. Find a place where the waters mix. Everyone, put on your swimsuits; bring drinking water and a towel."

I felt sorry for the folks already relaxing in the hot spring when our troop showed up. We avoided the scalding water and found a nice mix. Dravinaksha had been here before. I sat near him in pleasantly hot water. We chatted about days gone by while the youth created their own memories, dunking and splashing one another. Tourists observed our group, commenting in German or Chinese or a number of other languages.

The cold-water side of the river was dangerously fast-flowing. The kids had to try it. The others shouted, "No don't go! *No*! You'll get swept away!"

"I'm good, it's OK. I'm jumping in!"

"No! Don't do it! We love you!"

Splash. "Oh my god! It is *fareekan cold*! You gotta try it!"

This was repeated by several others. Other tourists followed, likely shouting similar comments on the icy cold in their own languages.

ᘓᘓᘓᘓᘓᘓ

Breakfast was peanut-butter oatmeal. Manorama told us that the first explorers considered this place evil. The volcanic activity made it useless for agriculture—in some places the ground gave away and the explorers dropped into super hot underground stuff and died instantly.

"Stay on the trail!" Manorama reminded us.

He pointed to the hill behind us.

"We're going to hike up there. Stay on the boardwalk." He cupped his hands around his mouth and repeated, "Again, follow the signs and stay on the trail! If you melt, we will not be able to bring you home, and your parents will miss you."

Dravinaksha and I looked at a sign at the beginning of the trail—a drawing of a screaming kid falling through the ground with steam coming out of his knees. I pointed to a red baseball hat on the sand beyond the boardwalk. "Someone must have gone off the path."

"Yeah." Dravinaksha said, "and that's all that's left of him."

"I don't think it's one of ours—I don't recognize the hat."

ꗞꗞꗞꗞꗞꗞ

Old Faithful was on the opposite side of the park. We made it there with all our passengers.

Manorama explained how geysers work. He pointed to several others in the area. "Old Faithful is the most reliable. It goes up every fifty minutes. We're just in time to catch it. This will be one more item to check off your bucket list."

"I assume this fence is here to keep the geyser from walking around?" one of the British girls asked.

"Where would a geyser want to go?" I asked.

"Snack bar, maybe? Or Denver?"

Our group posed for a picture as Old Faithful erupted.

That night, Parikshit stayed awake with me as I drove.

"Many years ago," I said, "they put me in jail here in Billings."

"Billings?"

"It's the biggest city in Montana. We were selling *Bhagavad-gitas,* and someone called the police. They thought we were aliens, like other-planet aliens. It was 1978. The police took me in for a while, then let me go. The other devotees in the van had no idea where I'd gone. There were no cell phones back then."

"How did they find you?"

"I called the temple from a pay phone. Do you know what that is, a pay phone?"

"I've heard of them."

"Three of us lived in a van. We were about your age. How old are you?"

"Twenty-one," said the voice in the dark.

"Yeah, same age. We went cross-country selling books, stopping at temples to reload. What do you think? Would you like that? Travel, sell books, go to jail?"

"Yeah, it sounds good. I think I'd better finish college first."

CHAPTER 18

Llamas and
Fortune Tellers

The local Mormons are proud of their Krishna temple, with its traditional Indian architecture, and local visitors come to pet the llamas and climb the steps to the temple balcony, where they can point to their homes in the distance.

Downstairs, in the temple restaurant, bus tour kids were watching Vaibhavi talk with her parrot. Vaibhavi noticed me walk in. "I was wondering when I was going to see you," she said.

"I'm glad you're still with us," I said. She had had cancer a few years ago.

"It takes a lot to stop me. Hey, tell these kids to start

buying stuff. It costs a lot of money to run this place." She turned her attention back to the parrot.

"Her husband, Charu, was my temple president back in 1976." I told the kids.

"1976?" They looked at me as if I were a museum exhibit.

"Vaibhavi and Charu are a powerful team. They designed and built a temple in Australia, then moved to the US and settled in Berkeley. Have you seen the temple there? No? You're going to—it's on our tour. Then they came here and built this place. They never had kids." I motioned to the building around us, "*This* is their kid—and it's their third."

Vaibhavi called across the room, "I've got some llama shears." She pointed to Radha Vinode's big Afro. "We could take care of that for you."

Radha Vinode replied in his polite British voice, "Oh, thank you, Mataji, but I'll be keeping this today. Thank you, though."

"No, I don't mind," Vaibhavi said. "I'll run and get them right now. It will be a big improvement."

Radha Vinode looked uneasy.

The conversation was interrupted by Jaya Sri Radhe doing her five-clap—one, *two;* one, two, *three*—and the bus tour kids echoed her, clap, *clap,* clap-clap *clap.*

Jaya Sri Radhe announced, "We'll be performing tonight; get your costumes and makeup ready. Tomorrow we'll ride horseback through a Navajo Indian reservation. This is Vaibhavi. She and her husband, Charu, built this beautiful place. As you know, they have the festival of colors here every year. Over thirty thousand people dance in kirtan and throw colors on each other. They've asked if we can help in their garden. How many of you can help with pulling weeds?"

A few hands went up.

"That's pretty good." Vaibhavi said, "But we can use a lot more help. C'mon you guys. You have to work for your lunch."

A few more hands went up.

"You have to work for your lunch."

Vaibhavi caught Radha Vinode's eye and made a scissors motion with her fingers. Radha Vinode's eyes grew large. No one noticed or asked what I was laughing at.

൸൸൸൸൸൸

An elderly man from India read everyone's palms. The crowd moved in close to listen. "This line is your life," he said, peering through his thick glasses. "You're going to live sixty-six years. You will have seven children." The crowd cheered. "And this line, uh"—he looked through a magnifying glass—"you will not have much money, but you are intelligent, very intelligent." The crowd cheered again.

"Who's next? Oh you've been sitting here, waiting. What is your name? Do you have a man in mind, a boy to marry?"

"No," the young lady said.

"Good. You should wait"—he looked at the side of her hand—"until you're twenty-eight. The first man you meet, don't marry him. Wait till you meet the second man. The first one will be no good." He dropped her hand, "OK, who's next?"

He examined the next girl's hand. "You're a jewel in your family!"

"Really?" She was skeptical after hearing her friend's report.

"Yes! You'll bring fame and wealth to your family. They're very fortunate to have you. See this line right here?"

"Yes."

"It's very clear."

"What's very clear?"

"This line."

"Yes it is. But what does it mean?"

"It's very clear."

"Yes. Thank you. What does it mean?"

"Your parents must be proud of you."

"Yes, I think they are—"

I went for a walk.

When I returned, the palm reader called me over. After glancing at my hand he happily announced I would die at fifty-four.

"I'm fifty-eight right now," I said.

He looked at my hand again. "Perhaps there was a health crisis at fifty-four?"

"No."

He looked disappointed.

"I'm sorry about that," I said, "I really am."

๚๚๚๚๚๚

Narayan kept me awake as I drove through Arizona that night.

"What did you think of the palm reader?"

Narayan laughed, "That guy was a joke."

"I agree. He said I died four years ago."

"He got one thing right, though. He said I would accomplish anything I set my mind to. Like an arrow shot by a warrior, nothing will stop it."

"That's encouraging. I hope he's right."

"I pride myself in never starting something I can't finish."

"And I pride myself in starting projects that are so awesome and epic that no one will ever finish them."

The sound of the bus's tires roaring across the Arizona pavement was the only response.

CHAPTER 19

A Bus with No Air

If you get hurt on an Indian reservation, it's your own problem; you're responsible for yourself. There were no helmets if you fell off your horse, and no waivers to sign.

My horse lagged behind our group. "Kick him," the guide said, "kick him hard." That was my only riding instruction.

Canyon De Chelly looks like a miniature Grand Canyon designed by Salvador Dalí. Our guide pointed to an old cliff dwelling that had been abandoned hundreds of years ago. We weren't allowed to get close to it, though. Our horses pawed the ground, snorted, and bit each other as the guide talked, and then we turned around to head back.

The horses were suddenly in a hurry when we changed direction. I pushed my hat down hard and hung on tight.

On an Indian reservation, no one minds when beginners gallop across the desert sand hooting and shouting, but when Aravinda fell off his horse, our guide chased the horse down and brought it back to him. "This one likes to stop like that," the guide said. "Be careful." When the horse tried it again, Aravinda impressed the Navajo by staying in his saddle.

꽨꽨꽨꽨꽨꽨

"Dad. Do you want to hike into the Grand Canyon?"

"You woke me up with such a dumb question? Of course I do."

"We're leaving right away. Before it gets hot."

"OK, thank you."

There was no air conditioning in the bus; morning was the only time I'd be able to sleep in the desert heat. We'd driven all night and we'd be driving the next couple of nights. Still, we assembled in the cool morning darkness. "Drink plenty of water or you'll die," Manorama told everyone. "Hike down as far as you want until seven-thirty, then head back up. It will get hot very quickly."

Morning twilight revealed the canyon as we descended into it, legs sore from our horseback riding.

I was asked to follow the slow hikers—girls in fashionable shoes. We heard the rest of our troupe zigzag down the trail below us, singing their way into the canyon.

The sun rose and the vista brightened. "Wow! Look at that!" one of the girls said. "Can we stop here for a while?"

"Sure. We're in no hurry. Take your time, look around. Look up there where we came from. Do you see those people?"

"Whoa! We were all the way up there?"

"Yep, and we have to walk back up again."

"Let's go a little further down. It really looks interesting."

"OK," I replied, "but remember, we have to climb back up. It's already getting warm. People die here every day."

"Every day?"

"Isn't that what Manorama said?"

The girls mostly talked with one another about makeup techniques, school stuff, and famous people I'd never heard of as they walked. I was happy to be in the Grand Canyon with cheerful people who encouraged each other and giggled a lot.

One of the delicate shoes broke. "You guys keep going," its owner said. "I don't want you to stop because of me."

The other girls wouldn't allow that. "We'll stay here with you."

"Aww, really?"

"You can go on ahead Mitra Prabhu. We'll be all right."

"This is the only thing Manorama asked me to do: to

stay behind the slowest hiker, to make sure we get everyone back. So I'm OK. There's a nice view here. Let's eat our snacks. There's no point carrying them back up the hill."

We took in the view as we ate our energy bars and oranges and drank some of our water. Chipmunks appeared. The girls tossed them bits of their snacks and declared that chipmunks were the cutest things they'd ever seen.

It was different from being with the boys. Our boys were pleasant, but no matter how hard they tried, they couldn't be as girly as the real thing.

"I have some nostalgia for this place," I said. "I stayed here for a month when I was about your age."

"When was that?" The girls asked.

"1977." I again felt like a museum exhibit. "I'm older than these rocks."

"Really?"

"Not by much," I said.

We heard singing from the trail below—several voices singing together.

"Is that—?" one of the girls asked.

We listened carefully.

"It's Parikshit," she said. "You can hear his voice over everyone else's."

"It is!"

The hikers appeared around the bend below us, Parikshit leading the way, marching briskly up the hill, singing with his stage-projection voice, "*Jaya jaya gaurachander arotika shobha!*"

The rest of his group echoed the line, also at full

volume. It's a national park, I thought. People come here for quiet and solitude, and here's a bunch of noisy Hare Krishna kids.

Hikers smiled and made room for them on the trail.

The singing boys marched past us.

The girls said goodbye to the chipmunks then picked their way up the trail, one with a bare foot.

"Watch your step."

"It's sort of like a broken sidewalk in a rough part of town."

"But with a nice view."

"Yes."

It was hot on the bus. Not humid like Houston—this was Grand Canyon desert heat—no shade trees, only rocks to store the heat. I looked at the map. There would be no relief from the desert that day. Our bus had no air conditioning.

Kaliyaphani was talking with Manorama, his face red and his eyes wild. "I came on this tour to escape the Florida heat. This is"—he lifted his hands as he searched for the word—"unbearable! I can't take it any longer."

Manorama apologized.

"I've had it," Kaliyaphani said. "I'm leaving at the next stop to wherever there's air conditioning."

After the meeting Manorama said, "Try to get some sleep today, Mitra Prabhu."

"In a toaster? Sure!" I tried to be as cheerful as the girls had been.

Manorama smiled.

"I'm sorry. That's all we have."

I found a bit of shade under a cactus, but I didn't last long there.

ௐௐௐௐ

It was the hottest time of the year in the hottest part of America. Our bus was the only vehicle on Interstate 40 with open windows. Kaliyaphani drove as we sat in the back, shirts off, shouting over the road noise while sheets and towels blew in the wind.

"How are you holding up?" I asked. "Have you seen anything like this in England?" The heat was a curiosity for them, something to write home about.

They were also curious to read the *Srimad-Bhagavatam*. They'd heard from it while growing up in temple communities. "This will be different," I told them. "*You're* giving the class today. I want to hear each of you say something in your own words, anything that you understand."

Each boy took a turn reading, pausing when passing trucks were too loud.

The story was older than the surrounding rock formations. Sage Narada was telling the story of his previous life. When he'd been a child, a group of sages had stayed at his home. He listened to their stories, which had had such an influence on him that when his mother died, he had been able start his spiritual quest and fend for himself.

Parikshit's voice rose above the traffic sounds as he read from the *Bhagavatam*: "I took this as the special mercy of the Lord, who always desires benediction for His devotees, and so thinking, I started for the north."

"How do you do that?" one boy asked. "It's like you've got a built-in microphone."

"Later—I'll show you later," Parikshit answered. "Let's keep reading."

"Yes," I said. "Can you read the commentary with your built-in microphone?"

"Certainly." Parikshit continued, "Confidential devotees of the Lord see in every step a benedictory direction of the Lord. What is considered to be an odd or difficult moment in the mundane sense is accepted as special mercy of the Lord."

"What did you get from that?" I asked.

"All situations are a blessing."

"Do you really believe that?" I asked.

"In theory. I'd like to."

"It's a challenge."

Each had something to say, even the quiet ones. Their parents had prayed to have children with an appetite for wisdom. I supplied questions, then stepped back to listen.

"Some situations are really hard, and you wonder why Krishna's putting me through this."

"But He's always got it under control. It's not beyond Him."

"And He's looking out for us …"

"So," I asked, "is *every* moment significant? Or is it only the tough ones?"

"Yes, I suppose that's where we're supposed to be going with this. Every moment is sacred."

"Even the moments when we're flitting about?"

"Exactly."

"Shall we read more?"

"Yes, let's."

"The child Narada wandered alone through cities, towns, forests, mining areas. He sat by a lonely river to meditate, searching for God in his heart."

They passed the book around the circle.

"As soon as I began to meditate, tears rolled down my eyes and without delay Sri Krishna appeared on the lotus of my heart. Being overpowered by feelings of happiness, every part of my body became separately enlivened, I could not see both myself and the Lord. Upon losing that form, I suddenly got up, being perturbed, as is usual when one loses that which is desirable."

"Should we keep reading?" I asked. "It's been over an hour."

"We can't just leave him there."

"I'd better get some sleep," I said, "Kaliyaphani is staying in Las Vegas; I'll have to drive all night by myself."

"We'll keep reading and let you know how the story goes."

"I'd like that. Good night everyone."

ಌಌಌಌಌಌ

With the enthusiasm of a new convert, Dustin gave me a tour of the building site for the new Las Vegas temple.

"I hope it moves quickly," I said. I'd seen projects start with a bang, then stagnate with multiple opinions.

"We've got a good team," Dustin said.

The temple team had rented an office space for their

temporary temple at the industrial park right next door to the building site.

Our bus kids filled the office/temple, and volunteers fed us dinner. I chose watermelon.

"We are your servants," they said. "Take as much as you want."

My plate heavily laden, I picked my way through the room. Each kid had to scoot out of my way before I found enough room to sit. The boys looked at my plate.

"In the *Bhagavad-gita* Krishna clearly says, 'I am the taste of watermelon.'"

"Does he really say that?"

"Yes, 'I am the taste of water.' I'm convinced He meant to say watermelon but was in a hurry." I held up a slice, admiring the color. "This is what we need after driving across the desert in a bus with no air—hey, isn't there a song like that?"

Mali sang, "I drove through the desert on a bus with no air."

"Oh great," I said. "It took me forty years to get that song out of my head."

A couple of boys joined him in harmony, "La la, la la la la la—and in the desert, you can remember your name, 'cause there ain't no one for to give you no pain."

"How do you know all these songs from my era? You know them better than I do."

Dustin squeezed into our little group. He had philosophy questions, but I needed to focus on watermelon.

"On our drive today," I said, "our group read a chapter of *Srimad-Bhagavatam*. Let's hear each of you say what you remember. Mali? Can you start?"

"I'll try," Mali said. "Vyasadeva was sitting in meditation in Badarik Ashram, or the ashram of *badari* berries. He'd written down all of the Vedas, yet felt unfulfilled."

Our section hushed to hear Mali's recitation.

"Vyasadeva's guru, Narada, appeared and said you've got to make your message clear and simple, and you need to tell it as a story to be effective. Narada told the story of his previous life as an example of how stories motivate people."

"This is so interesting," Dustin said. "I want to read the book now."

"Life doesn't get much better than this," I said. "Watermelon and *Bhagavatam* at the same time."

"Should I go on?" Mali said.

"Keep going if you have more," I said. "Tell us everything you remember."

"Yes, keep going." The Las Vegas team sat with us. "You're bringing the story to life!"

Mali described Narada's progress through the stages of bhakti, culminating in seeing the Lord in his heart, then hearing His voice. "'Since then I've achieved this spiritual body with complete freedom. Whenever I chant about the Lord, he appears on the seat of my heart, as if called for. All this came about by my hearing stories from sages.' That's the kind of story Vyasadeva should write."

We were about to applaud, but Manorama made an announcement. "Everyone get back on the bus. Get your things. Don't leave anything behind—we're not coming back!"

It had been a full day hiking the Grand Canyon, riding across the desert in a hot bus, then visiting the Las Vegas temple. But there was one more event: the kids would sing Hare Krishna on the neon streets of Las Vegas.

Kaliyaphani handed me his bus key. "I'll see you in Los Angeles." He looked relieved.

"We'll drive him to Los Angeles," the Las Vegas team said.

"Make sure it's a refrigerated car."

"We're your servants. Whatever you need."

Kaliyaphani smiled. The song "Bus with No Air" played on in my head.

CHAPTER 20

California

Narottam and I recited *Bhagavad-gita* verses from memory to stay awake for the overnight drive to San Diego. "You're such a weirdo," I said with affection, "learning all that Sanskrit. I wish there were more people like you."

᠁᠁᠁

Our first stop that morning was the Pacific Ocean. We caught a few waves, then walked to the temple, which is just a couple of blocks from the beach. Lunch was in the courtyard under tropical trees that broke the sunlight into dancing palm-leaf triangles.

The Pacific Ocean keeps San Diego cool in summer and warm in winter. The weather there made me wonder why I'd chosen to live in North Carolina all these years.

Our bus tour kids were beautiful and well dressed. I tried to blend in by standing tall and thinking young.

Nitya Lila was at the head of the line, making plates.

"You're serving again?" I asked.

"Yes, I enjoy it!"

"Then I'll eat something to make you happy."

"That's a good idea. Take one more of these."

I hope to live long enough to see these kids take over the world.

A monk joined me at the table. "Do you remember me?" he said.

"Yes, of course! But from where?"

"We met in Seattle a few years back."

"Oh, yes! You're from Iran."

"Yes."

"You read the *Gita* in Iran."

"Yes."

"Then you met devotees at Penn State University."

"Yes."

"Then got a job in Seattle. When I met you there, you said the devotees were the only people you knew—your entire social circle."

"Yes."

"So now you're here? A full time monk?"

"Yes."

Our table was loud with jokes and conversations, so I leaned in closer to be heard. "That required teamwork," I said. "Someone brought a book to Iran. Was that risky?"

"Yes, it was."

"You found it and became interested."

"More than interested. I was hungry, searching."

"Then you met devotees in America several times. It was a team that got you from one point to the next."

"Yes. I'm grateful to each of them."

"We each play a part."

Laughter erupted at our table, migrated to the other tables, and suddenly it was too loud for us to talk anymore. We ate our lunches and watched the fun.

৩৩৩৩৩৩

As I locked the bus, an elderly woman in colorful clothes stopped to admire it. "I lived many happy years in a bus just like this," and her eyes brightened.

I told her about our tour.

"It's wonderful that young people still do that!"

"Yes."

Then she asked, "What are you about? I've seen you people over the years."

"We believe in kindness." I'd never answered this question in this way before, but it felt right. "I've been sustained by kindness, and I pass it on every chance I get." I held up my guitar, "I'm supposed to be at the temple right now. There's a concert. You're welcome to join."

"I just might."

We parted. I walked quickly, hoping to be in time for the sound check. The conversation had given me a motto, something to live by. I hoped to put it into practice—letting kindness flow through me.

It was getting dark; restaurants were crowded with laughter and songs. I walked faster, past couples enjoying the California night scene, the weather, the music. In a shadow, a young man sat on his guitar case, tears streaming as he wailed, then buried his head between his knees. His shoulders shook as he sobbed.

Homeless people are everywhere in California. People rush by so they won't become homeless themselves—and that rushing let's them bypass their emotions. I walked past with everyone else. People were counting on me at the temple.

But the street singer's cry haunted me as we sang that night. My prayers felt empty; I was a hypocrite. After the show, the same young man appeared in front of the temple. The girls surrounded him with sympathy, and Nitya Lila brought him something to eat.

ꛁꛁꛁꛁꛁꛁ

Venice Beach, Los Angeles

A guy in Bedouin robes played an electric guitar while roller-skating past vendors and magic shows. A juggler started the engines on three chain saws.

The main event that day would be the Hare Krishna Ratha Yatra festival. Festival of India tents were supplemented with more tents and stages. Venice Beach is always busy, but on festival day the crowd doubles.

My California Krishna friends know their craft: they know how to reach people through art and music. I can fix a tractor or build a house, but what use is a slow-talking country boy in L.A.?

I watched a friend answer questions before an audience of two hundred. When did he get so good at this? I would have fumbled around for half an hour trying to find my words. He was eloquent in the speed of L.A. The more I watched, the more humbled I became. It's good to feel empty and useless occasionally. It doesn't particularly *feel* good, but it clears space for learning.

I stepped aside to let a suntanned guy ride by on his bike, a twelve-foot piece of driftwood balanced on his shoulder, and then I took my place in line for the free feast. A young man complimented my hat.

"Oh, thank you. Are you a local?"

"No, I'm from Santa Barbara." He removed his sunglasses. "I came here hoping to find books on bhakti yoga."

"I might be able to help you."

He took up the rest of my day. I was glad to feel useful again.

ௐௐௐௐ

Bus tour kids packed up tents as the sun sank into the Pacific Ocean. The bicycle guy helped, still balancing his

piece of driftwood and also asking questions about the *Bhagavad-gita*.

፴፴፴፴፴

In Yosemite, we parked the buses under sequoia trees, and Manorama announced, "Line up for lunch and snacks. We leave for Bridalveil Fall in ten minutes. Bring towels and swim clothes."

Nitya Lila handed out lunch packets. "This is a bean burrito, this one is cheese, and everyone gets one of these and a dessert."

Our group headed up the mountain with day packs. I took the rear, helping stragglers. "Just put one foot in front of the other—you're doing fine. See that cliff up there? That's where we're going."

The trail followed a river with pounding water and mist from waterfalls. Signs warned us to stay off the slippery rocks. "There's a lot of dangerous stuff here. Stay on the trail and you'll get to see it. But if you fall, can I have your snacks?"

The group lingered at the top. The waterfall covered Narayan's voice as he pointed across the valley. Since he's an Eagle Scout, I assumed he was teaching woodlore.

The thundering waterfall and majestic view was an appropriate place for my Tarzan yell. I gave it all I had. Narayan looked concerned. "Dad?"

I let out another yell so he'd know I was fine.

Then I joined his little group, "Glaciers passed through here and made these valleys with steep rock faces like what we just hiked up. The last time I came here I was eight. The whole time I was worried the glaciers would pass through again and crush us. I was disappointed when we saw a real one."

"Yeah, they just kinda sit there."

The top of the mountain was flat; a chunk of granite with a river running across it and trees popping up here and there—very different from anything I'd seen in North Carolina or Florida.

We assembled at a small lake that had been carved from the granite—like a stone bowl. "We'll have lunch here," Manorama said, "and you can go swimming. Just don't go downstream. The current will throw you over the edge, and we'll have to pick you up at the bottom and put your pieces in little plastic bags to mail to your mother."

The cold water knocked the wind out of us. We swam to the other side to lie on a granite slab which had been warmed by the sun. After several freeze/thaw cycles, the kids noticed that the river , as it flowed into the lake, had worn the stone slab smooth enough to slide down.

ௐௐௐௐௐ

Amal joined the tour in L.A. as the designated kirtan singer. Since all the kids sang well, I wondered what purpose he served in particular. Amal sat on the blue tarp

Crater Lake

between the two buses with the rest of us, singing under the stars. He'd sung for years in the holy town of Vrindavan, learning from the best, absorbing the mood of sweetly calling out.

The kirtan was majestic, like Yosemite. Amal stayed with us for the rest of the tour.

ௐௐௐௐௐ

After swimming in Crater Lake, we drove our buses to the top of Mount Rainier.

Mali and Radha Vinode

From my sleeping bunk, I heard Radha Vinode shout across the parking lot, "We're above the clouds! I always wanted to touch a cloud."

His voice came closer. "Oh no! Look! One of them is falling! The sky is falling! *The sky is falling!*" When he reached the door of the bus one of the boys said, "Shhh, Radha Vinode, look, you're making Mitra laugh."

His Afro appeared over my bunk. "Oh. Sorry."

I gave up on sleep. "Radha Vinode, I want to let you know how much I appreciate that you've kept the ceiling of the bus so clean."

His eyes and smile grew as he moved his hair across the ceiling, "Yes, I've been hard at it. Thanks for noticing."

"There's a little spot right there—"

"Oh, yes, I've been meaning to…"

᳇᳇᳇᳇᳇᳇

After a long hike, the blue tarp was spread over the mountaintop parking lot. With the Alpine scenery, our troupe looked like a scene from *The Sound Of Music*.

Jahnavi had a bag of lost and found items from the

girls' bus. She held up a shirt, "Whose is this?" The item was claimed.

"Whose shorts are these?"

"Oh, they're mine," Mali said.

Jahnavi tossed them to him. "Mali, you shouldn't be leaving your shorts on the girls' bus."

From that point, all unclaimed items were assigned to Mali, who calmly replied, "Oh yes, mine. Sorry." The pile of girls' clothes continued to grow in front of him until Nitya Lila brought a steaming pot from the bus. "Get your plates."

We enjoyed an elegant meal on the blue plastic tarp.

CHAPTER 21

Vancouver

Vancouver's Krishna temple had been built on a peat bog, so the parking lot has melted into the soft ground and the lampposts hang at random angles. "It's like a Salvador Dalí painting."

Grappa looked through the bus window. "Dalí? The one with the melting watches?"

"Yes," I said. "He'd be inspired here."

"This landscape *does* look rather surreal," Grappa replied. "Did you sleep well?"

"Best ever. I slept six hours Canadian."

"Canadian?"

"You know, like Canadian dollars and American dollars?"

"Ah, yes. And which is worth more?"

"Canadian hours are worth more because I feel rested, eh?"

I sent a report to my email group about our Yosemite experiences, and several people replied with questions and congratulations. Names were being added every day to my email group as old and new friends wanted to stay in touch.

ௐௐௐௐௐௐ

Ratha Yatra festivals are held every Saturday throughout the summer. Our tour followed the festival route, filling the days in between with national parks and beaches.

Vancouver's Ratha Yatra began with a parade of bagpipes, politicians, and clowns on roller skates. These attracted a crowd to watch the enthusiastic kirtan before the Jagannath Ratha Yatra chariot. The public was then invited to help pull the ropes or follow the parade to Stanley Park.

A sunburned girl handed me a hundred-dollar bill.

"I saw your email," she said, "and want to support what you're doing."

"But how did you—?"

"I read between the lines. I know what you and Maharha are going through."

"But—you guys are struggling too."

"That won't stop us from helping something we like."

"Thank you. I want to do this full-time."

"I know. And there's a need for what you do. Can we get you and Maharha to fly out here sometime?"

"I never turn down an opportunity."

A cool breeze blew across Stanley Park. Noses and cheeks grew redder as the day progressed.

On stage, the bus tour girls performed their traditional dance, which drew a large crowd. Backstage, an Indian woman praised their performance to me as I tuned my guitar.

Radha Vinode shouted into the microphone, "That was *spectacular*, wasn't it? Let's give them one more massive round of applause!" He held the audience while the stage was set up. "We're traveling in a bus all over North America. We've come from England, Ireland, India, and some are all the way from Florida! Now we're going to perform a bit of kirtan for you. We're almost ready. Are you ready yet? Yes, they're almost ready, so just hang on a bit, another moment, and we'll begin straightaway."

I felt the bill in my pocket. Someone believed in me.

CHAPTER 22

Krishna Farm, Ashcroft, British Columbia

Two hours before sunrise I drove the bus past the sign welcoming us to Saranagati.

Deep in the Canadian wilderness, Saranagati is a five-mile-long valley owned by Hare Krishna families. I parked the bus and took a nap, waking in time for pancakes smothered in Canadian maple syrup.

Manorama made announcements while I ate. "For lunch, we'll meet at a house over there." He pointed to a forest across the road. "You have two hours to find it, but *don't* walk alone—there are a lot of bears."

I walked down the gravel road with my prayer beads.

A farm truck appeared, followed by a dust cloud. The driver was happy to see a visitor. We talked about crops as I peeled the orange I had saved from breakfast.

He pointed, "Saranagati extends as far as you see up this valley. Several families pitched in to buy it many years ago."

I looked for a polite place to throw the orange peel.

"I'll take it," the driver said. He put the peel in a plastic bag and zipped it shut. "A bear will smell that for miles and come looking."

In the distance, something moved toward us.

"It's one of the girls," the farmer said.

"She's really going fast."

"It's an electric booster on her bike."

"To outrun bears?"

The girl stopped at the truck, breathing hard. "Where are they?" She looked about thirteen. "Where is everyone?"

"Up that way;" I pointed, "the house on the right."

"The community house?"

"Yeah. They'll be there a little longer then they're going to—"

She pushed off without looking back, "OK, Haribol!"

"This must be a big day for her."

"They've been looking forward to it all year."

"I can imagine. Whenever the bus came to our place in North Carolina it was a big deal. We're remote, but you guys are a five hour drive from nowhere."

◊◊◊◊◊◊

The bus tour kids were more attentive than usual as

the bicycle girl showed them around the log house. "The floorboards were milled here—we have our own sawmill."

"And you grow your own food?"

"We have a big garden. We grow a lot of our own."

"What's this room for?"

"It's a greenhouse for starting plants."

"How cold does it get?"

"Minus twenty, sometimes minus forty. But when you're outside cutting wood, you'd be surprised. It's not that bad."

"You get to live here year round?" one of the boys asked. "This is the best part of the whole tour."

The bicycle girl smiled at the floor.

Narayan played Turkish Rondo on the piano in the living room.

"Man! Is there any instrument you don't play?"

He smiled and let Manorama take a turn.

Chaitanya arrived with lunch. She was a few years older than the bicycle girl, perhaps eighteen. Everyone called her Chay.

"Wow! Is this stuff you guys grew here?"

"We don't grow pizzas on this farm," Chay said.

Nitya Lila helped organize the serving table, and the rest of us lined up.

"Why is this so good?"

"It was cooked in a wood-fired clay oven."

"And this salad—it's the best!"

A dark form moved on the fence around the garden.

"What is that?"

"Oh my god! It's a bear! Right over there! *A bear!*"

The bear pulled branches from a tree and ate the

leaves, paying no attention to the kids who set their pizzas down to get their cameras.

"Awww, he's so cute."

We were close enough to see insects flying around the bear's head. Kids stepped off the porch for a better look.

"Uh, guys?" Manorama said. "Take a hint from the locals. Notice they're all on the porch."

They glanced at the porch and back to the bear. "But he's so cute."

"Yes, but you won't look cute if you get in his way. We'll have to mail you back to your mothers in tiny plastic bags."

The kids took one step back. "Awww, look at that. He's so cute."

They ignored my Yogi Bear imitation, "Hey Boo Boo! Whaddayagot in that pic-a-nic basket, Boo Boo?"

I asked Chay, "What do you do when a bear gets in your garden?"

"I chase them out. You have to. Here, take some more pizza."

I took some. "I don't argue with girls who chase bears."

꒩꒩꒩꒩꒩

Smiling through his beard, Bala Krishna pointed to his hydroelectric turbine.

"This has been spinning nonstop for fifteen years. It powers four houses."

He turned a valve and the turbine doubled its speed. "We'll need more power with all the company we're having tonight."

"The water comes from up on that mountain?"

"Yeah, there's a spring we tap into. It comes down these hoses and builds up pressure." He pointed to a gauge, "One hundred sixty pounds of pressure."

"Wow, that's a lot."

"It goes through this turbine, then it waters my fields." Bala Krishna makes a living from farming.

௹௹௹௹௹

More families arrived, filling his yard with bicycles and rusty trucks. They brought pots and more kids. A table full of farm-fresh food was served as the sun set behind the mountain.

"What's been grown here?" I asked, as they loaded my plate.

"Carrots, squash, beans, and tomatoes are from the farm. The milk is from a local organic dairy. The beets are also from the garden."

"This is too good to eat in the dark." I turned on my flashlight. "Look at these colors."

Bala Krishna sat with a bucket and a flashlight. "Who wants raspberry ice cream?"

A line formed.

He asked an eight-year-old, "Are you the kind of girl who likes raspberry ice cream?"

"Yes."

"Well, you have to say it without smiling so I know you're serious. Are you serious about wanting ice cream?"

"Yes, I am."

"You're smiling, though. You have to be serious."

Bus tour kids began their kirtan magic by candlelight. Bala Krishna gave me a second scoop of the best raspberry ice cream I'd ever had. "This house never sleeps," he said. "It's always like this. My wife and I joke that maybe we should move back to Vancouver for peace and quiet."

CHAPTER 23

Golden Moments with Pinocchio

"Dad! There's a really nice view down that trail."

I'd just woken up and was trying to remember where we were.

"You've got to see it!"

" It takes a lot to impress me. I'm from Hawaii."

"You'll like it."

I followed the trail to Lake Louise, where people paddled canoes over turquoise water framed by steep mountains. One mountain jutted into the lake, making you wonder what those faraway people in canoes saw as they rounded the bend.

Bus kids laughed. "It doesn't look real. It's too nice."

"Rocks, dirt, trees, water—the same stuff we see everywhere," I said, "but this is like a good cook who can make a miracle dish from potatoes."

"Someone did a good job."

"This is fairy tale stuff. Where are the unicorns?"

"It's like there's a painting behind the lake."

"It's fake," I said. "Nothing can look this nice."

Manorama got everyone into their bus-tour tee shirts for a group photo in front of the lake. Narayan and I stood in the back with the other tall people.

"OK everyone—don't squint—one, two, three! OK, one more!"

"We'll meet for lunch up on that mountain," Manorama pointed. "There's another lake up there. Everyone, take your time and enjoy the hike."

We zigzagged through forests of deep green pines.

"Grappa," I said, "look at that hat Jayananda's wearing."

"It's much too small for him," Grappa said.

Jayananda's Irish nose had been getting redder every day. He'd borrowed a hat to protect it.

"With those shorts—" I said, as Jayananda bounced ahead through the pines. "We're in a magic forest where Pinocchio's become a *real boy*!"

"Hey, Jayananda," Grappa said, "you'd better be careful not to tell any lies."

Jayananda aimed his red nose at us. "What's that?"

"You'd better not tell any lies."

"All right, then." Jayananda turned and bounced along the trail while Grappa and I walked like puppets.

"Hey, Jayananda," Grappa called again, "you look like Pinocchio."

Jayananda looked back.

"It's the hat, and your shorts."

Jayananda pulled at the legs of his shorts, curtsied, tipped his hat, and continued bouncing over the rocky trail.

ᘓᘓᘓᘓᘓᘓ

We were greeted by a caribou at Jasper Park.

"Look at those antlers," I said.

"You don't want to mess with that guy."

"I'm not getting off the bus till he's gone."

We slept under the open sky to watch the meteor shower due that night.

Chay had joined our tour for a week. I watched her build the fire—she knew what she was doing. "We'll be safe from any bears with Chay here."

We circled around the fire and took turns singing.

Chay surprised the boys with her mridanga playing, and they applauded when she finished.

᳇᳇᳇᳇᳇᳇

The next morning Manorama announced, "Today we'll visit the hot springs—it's a forty-minute drive—then we'll come back here for dinner."

"You'll really like this," Sri Ram told me. He was the polite one, always holding doors open and running errands. "It's my favorite spot on the whole bus tour. The springs are up on a mountain and the scenery is stunning."

"Alright," I said. "You talked me into it."

We drove through Rocky-Mountain scenery and checked in at the hot springs. There were four swimming pools, each with water at a different temperature than the others. Lifeguards blew their whistles at our boys a few times when they got rowdy.

I sat in the hottest pool with the other bus drivers, our brahmin threads floating over our chests. In the late 1970s, Dravinaksha had driven Vishnujana Swami's bus, a mobile temple full of monks. They traveled across the US, bringing Krishna to remote places.

"The Radha Damodar party only lasted a few years," he said, "like the Pony Express. People are still enamored with the idea."

"Prabhupada really liked it," I said. "Back then we were the same age as these boys."

"Vishnujana made it work. People loved him. It didn't matter if we were in Texas or Nebraska, they'd melt whenever he sang or spoke."

"You did good this morning," I said. "That class you

gave at the campsite—I'm glad I was there to hear it. Manorama said it was historic. You've driven all these years, and that was the first time you gave a *Bhagavatam* class on the bus tour. I could see you were feeling it, and the kids were in there too."

"After a couple of weeks on the road, I get all softened up, you know? Kind of emotional. I read stuff and it touches me. I just tried to share a little of that."

"I talked with the kids later on. They appreciated what you said."

"Let's get out of here. I'm starting to melt."

The lifeguard blew his whistle again. We joined the boys in the cold-water pool. Sri Ram pointed. "Look at those mountains. It's like we're swimming in a postcard."

"How does he know about postcards?" Dravinaksha said. "Do people still use them?"

꘡꘡꘡꘡꘡

Breakfast had been a bowl of Captain Crunch, and lunch

had not been served, so we were anticipating our dinner. Then the rain hit. It followed the buses down the mountain to the campground. Our windshield wipers barely kept up.

We pulled into our parking spot, and Manorama radioed the boys' bus. "We're going to cook on the bus. We won't make a fire."

"Really?" I asked, "Are you sure?"

It grew steamy on our bus with the windows shut tight against the horizontal rain. The wind shook the bus. We were hungry—I could hear it in the boys' voices.

"Mitra Prabhu," Sri Ram said, "the boys in back asked what we're doing. Is there a plan?"

"We're waiting," I said. "That's what we do on bus tour. Hurry up or wait. When we're done waiting, we'll hurry again."

Sri Ram laughed politely and told the boys, "We're waiting."

Through the blurry windshield I saw two boys carrying a large pot. I opened the door, and the bus came to life.

"What do we have?"

Dripping wet, the two boys showed us a steaming pot of soup and a tray of bread.

"Is that *all*?"

"I'm frick*in' hungry!*" Pretty light language considering the situation.

We filled our bowls with soup, and Manorama radioed, "We need to hurry—"

੫੫੫੫੫੫

Shyam was my keeper-upper that night as I gave into griping. I said again, "There are two modes on a bus tour: hurry and wait. That's all we do." I instantly regretted it and tried to repair the statement. "But there are moments in between."

"And those are golden," Shyam said. "That's the price we pay. We have to hurry, and sometimes we wait, and sometimes we go hungry."

"Mm-hmm."

"And it's worth every bit." He meant it.

Shyam had beaten me at my own game. I'm supposed to be the adult with insight and a positive attitude. We'd been swimming in a postcard, and seen caribou, glaciers, and a meteor shower. You can't have *everything* in one day. It was a while before I could respond. "What are some golden moments for you?"

"There are so many."

"Pick one or two."

"At Saranagati, at Yamuna's house, when Amal led that kirtan—"

The bus hurried through the Canadian darkness to the next golden moment. I was still hungry, but at least it wasn't raining. I hope to live long enough to see what these kids do for the world.

CHAPTER 24

Unaccompanied Adult

At a truck stop somewhere in Montana, I found my bunk covered with stuff.

"It's mine, Dad," Narayan said. "I'm moving onto the girls' bus."

Manorama appeared at the door, "We're a day behind schedule. He has to catch his flight in Denver. The girls' bus is faster."

Boys climbed over me, squeezing by to visit the truck stop. Each of them asked, "What's going on?"

"Narayan's leaving us."

"What?"

"Oh no!"

"Don't leave us, Narayan!"

I stayed out of his way so he could pack.

Radha Vinode and Mali began a send-off kirtan in the parking lot, and other boys joined. They sang the Hare Krishna melody but with different words, "Narayan, Narayan. We're going to miss you, Narayan." Girls smiled down from the windows in the silver bus. It was a golden moment for my son.

He stepped down onto the greasy parking lot and set his bags down so we could hug. The boys circled us and echoed the girl's "Awwwwwww." Narayan was on his way to college.

"I'll see you in a couple of weeks, Dad."

卍卍卍卍卍卍

Manorama gave PJ a credit card. "There's no kitchen on your bus, so do your best to feed the boys. Be creative. It's a long, boring drive to Denver."

Although half my age, PJ is twice as responsible. He would help with the drive and keep everyone in line. The two of us shopped at a Costco, "I've got an idea," I said. "I've done this before when I had to cook without a stove."

We bought instant rice and mixed it with hot water at a truck stop. Cans of beans were poured into a bowl and mixed with spices and the rice, once it had softened. The boys were given tortillas and allowed to heap as much sour cream, avocados, lettuce, and chilis as they wanted to make themselves burritos.

They declared this to be the best meal ever, adding, "You guys should cook more often."

"Eat up," PJ said, "there's still plenty left."

꓿꓿꓿꓿꓿꓿

The next day, as I was driving through Wyoming, PJ's voice cut through the road noise: "Listen up, guys, we're stopping for fuel. Can one of you take care of the trash?" Mali raised his hand.

"And water?" Ananda volunteered.

"Who can dump the tanks?"

"My turn," Krishna Prema said. "I'll do it."

"And everyone else. Take care of your business quickly. Let's see how fast we can make it back out onto the road." I pulled up to the fuel station as PJ counted down.

"Five, four, three, two, one, *go!*"

He opened the door and checked his watch. "Can we do this in fifteen?"

Everyone jumped to their stations, and we were back on the road in record time. Once I had the bus on the open road I called Sri Ram over. "You guys did good. That took teamwork. Tell everyone I'm proud of them— pass it all the way to the back."

Sri Ram went to each boy and congratulated him. I heard Krishna Prema say, "Let's see if we can beat that time at the next stop."

They celebrated the golden moment with cold burritos and watermelon.

꓿꓿꓿꓿꓿꓿

In Denver I learned that Narayan had arrived in time to catch his flight. From that point on, I was an unaccompanied adult.

CHAPTER 25

Carlsbad Caverns, New Mexico

Our tour was almost over. I would be home in a week and I'd have to find work—maybe driving a freight truck. It was starting to weigh on me.

"Today we get to see Carlsbad Caverns," Manorama said. "One more item to check off your list. Bring warm clothes. It's fifty-seven degrees down there." We were sweating in the black asphalt parking area surrounded by cactus and the bus with no air.

Inside the visitor center Manorama announced, "We'll take the elevator 750 feet down. Once we're down there, read the signs and stay on the trail. Remember: sounds carry a long way in the cave, so don't shout—you're sup-posed to w-h-i-s-p-e-r."

ௐௐௐௐ

Deep underground there was a respectful silence, like an air-conditioned church. We came around a bend and the great room opened, "Oh my Krishna!" one of the girls whispered.

"Wow!"

"How did this happen?"

Manorama quietly repeated what the park ranger had said, "These stalactites grow about half an inch every eighty years."

"So that thing's really old."

We stayed on the path.

"If you touch the rocks, the ranger said, they stop growing."

Blobs of stone looked like giant people meeting un-der chandeliers. Signs on the walkway gave the various

formations creative names and explained how they were formed. A thousand feet underground, we saw the Chinese Theater, Soda Straws, and Drapery.

"This stuff is so weird," I whispered. "How do they design this stuff?"

Pranaya Keli said, "Krishna is an amazing artist."

"Do you really think Krishna designed this? It's just water dripping in a dark cave. Why would He give it so much attention? Who's going to see it?"

She shrugged. "It's no big deal for Him."

"OK. You talked me into it. Now it's even more amazing."

Krishna Prema tapped my shoulder. "We're supposed to meet by the elevator in about ten minutes."

"Oh, dang. It will take us that long just to get there."

"Yeah, we'd better turn back."

"We're never going to know what's around that bend." I pointed ahead.

"It's tempting."

"I think we can do it."

"If we walk fast."

೧೧೧೧೧೧

Back in the daylight, we thawed quickly. It was ninety degrees on the shady side of the bus.

While we ate dinner, Manorama announced, "We can leave right after we're done or watch the bats come out of the cave after dark. Is that something you'd like to see?"

"Bats! Yeah! Bats!"

Even the girls were into it. "Bats are cute. I *love* bats!"

೧೧೧೧೧೧

We joined the tourists who were finding seats in the bat arena. The ranger asked, "Does anyone know anything about bats? Anything at all? Yes, you over there." He passed a microphone to a five-year-old boy. The audience applauded his speech, and the ranger encouraged him to continue.

More tourists found their seats in the amphitheater, the sky darkened, and the ranger spoke about bats, their history, their challenges, how they fly, how they eat. He took off his hat, "How many do you think would fit in this hat?"

People suggested. "Ten? OK, that's a good guess. Anyone else? Twenty? That's a better guess, but keep going. Actually, it's seventy. They're not very big, and they're delicate. Little things affect their population: disease, weather, loss of habitat. This is one of the biggest bat swarms in the US. You're going to see something not available to many, so please," he whispered, "complete silence." Then he went back to his normal voice. "The bats have been flying out of this cave for centuries. We don't want to do anything to make them change their minds."

A couple of bats fluttered like butterflies. The ranger turned off his microphone and sat with two hundred silent tourists to watch the swarm. The ranger had said if we were lucky they'd fly close to us and we'd feel their wings beat the air over our head. Bats circled, climbed, gaining altitude to dive-bomb insects at high speed. Girls sighed, in love with three hundred thousand cute little bats.

ℛℛℛℛℛℛ

Walking back to the bus I said, "I had a question for the ranger, but he ran out of time."

"He knew a lot," Krishna Prema said. "What did you want to ask him?"

"I was going to ask him why Batman took off his cape."

"Is there an answer?"

"Of course. He had to go to the bat room."

CHAPTER 26

Key West, Florida

The Dallas devotees gave us a warm reception. There'd been thirteen new babies born in the community in the past year.

The next stop was the Krishna Farm in Mississippi, then a long haul to Key West, the last island on the chain off of Florida. We'd crossed a series of bridges the night before and stopped to watch the sun color the clouds as it set into the ocean. The next morning I woke to Radha Vinode saying, excitedly, "I can't believe it! Oh my god! It's a chicken, *and it's crossing the road*!"

We were going to reenact a moment of Key West history. A newspaper reporter took a photo of all of us posing before the bus, and we made the front page of the local paper. Dravinaksha was the star since he had been at the original event forty years ago.

Bus tour dining room

He'd been the bus driver when a team of Krishna monks sang at the pier each evening at sunset. Watching the sun set has always been part of the Key West social life. The Krishna people added live music all those years ago, and the tradition has continued. Since then, the area has built up with shops and tourists.

൝൝൝൝൝

Everyone dressed in their best Hare Krishna clothes. Dravinaksha confirmed, "This is the spot right here. This is where we sat with Vishnujana."

Tourists gathered and asked me when the show would start.

"It starts real soon," I said, "and you're part of it. Here's the words. Do you like to sing?"

"Sure!"

The girls started the kirtan. I pointed to the card, "Here's the words. When she's done singing, then it's our turn."

"Oh, OK! This looks fun!"

"It is. We've been all over North America this summer, and this is our last stop. We came all the way from Vancouver so you could sing with us."

The guy saluted the kirtan with his beer.

"OK, it's our turn, here we go—Hare Krishna, Hare Krishna, Krishna Krishna, Hare Hare …"

More people gathered, "What's this about?"

Tourists from China, Venezuela, and Idaho stayed past

sunset. Our troupe took the kirtan to the rest of town, where people in outdoor bars waved and cheered. They couldn't believe their good fortune to see a group of young Hare Krishnas bless their evening and they waved their drinks in appreciation.

෴෴෴

"I'll drive the first shift," PJ said. "Get some sleep. It's eight hours to Alachua."

I plugged in my Hearos, preparing for a long night. Florida is a great big state, and Key West is as far away as you can get from anything.

It started to rain. It rained so hard I heard it through my earplugs.

"Close *all* the windows," PJ shouted.

Followed by more shouting.

"It's hot!"

"Why can't we open the windows?"

"Duh, everything will get wet."

When it rained harder PJ pulled into a gas station. "I can't see," he shouted. "How can I drive?"

The boys watched the rain through the front window, then one of them said, "I want to go out there."

PJ smiled. "Put on your swimsuit. Go for it."

"Who wants to go with me?"

Everyone did.

I wanted to sleep but had to see what PJ was laughing at. Amal led a dozen boys into the downpour, stomping puddles to keep time, "*Radhe Radhe Radhe Barshane wali Radhe!*"[3] They danced, shirts off, laughing when the rain came down even harder. In the holy city of Vrindavan, Radha's devotees throw themselves into dancing with complete abandon.

It began as a joke, the boys waved their hands, gesturing in imitation, but they weren't laughing anymore. The tour was almost over, perhaps it was fatigue or egos worn smooth from travel—for a long moment they were carefree sadhus dancing in the headlights of the bus. "*Radhe Radhe Radhe Barshane wali Radhe!*"

When the rain stopped, cars at the gas station flashed their lights and honked in appreciation.

I returned to my bunk. "If I don't sleep, we're all going to die tonight."

୰୰୰୰୰୰

"Radha Vinode, you've got to keep me awake. What did you like best on the whole bus tour?"

"That kirtan in the rain!"

"You mean we could have bypassed everything else we did all summer?"

"It was a culmination."

---

3 *Radhe Radhe Radhe Barshane wali Radhe* — Radha who is very dear to Krishna comes from Varshana.

"And the main highlight for you."

"Yes, definitely."

"Now I feel sorry for everyone on the other bus."

"Yes, they missed it."

CHAPTER 27

Sugar Sand

People stood in a pond of clear water shouting at their kids as our troupe enjoyed the last day of the bus tour. We were at a park, only twenty miles from our final destination, the Alachua community.

I was in my element, chatting with locals about tractors and farming. I bragged about our tour. "We've been everywhere in the US and even into Canada putting on a show. These kids are really talented. A lot of them are from this area. Today's their homecoming; they're gonna put on their show for their families."

The locals offered me hamburgers from their grill.

"Thanks, I just ate."

"A beer? Cigarette?"

"I'm good, thanks. You know, some of these kids are from England."

"England? I ain't never—"

I called Mali over. "These people have never met an Englishman."

Mali extended his hand, "It's a pleasure, sir."

"D'ja have a good time?"

"Quite so." Mali smiled, "You've got a lovely country."

The locals nodded to each other and dragged on their cigarettes.

"It's been a pleasure to have met you." Mali shook their hands once more. "I'd best be running along."

It was time to hurry again—Manorama was calling out orders: "Everyone get into your costumes. If you're not in the drama, put on your best temple clothes. Boys, get on the bus and head to the temple so you can get the stage ready. We'll follow after we get lunch packed up."

I stayed to help pack the girls' bus. When we were done, Dravinaksha started the engine while Manorama closed the luggage compartments. Manorama cupped his hands, "OK, Drav, hit it."

The engine roared, the wheels spun, but the bus stayed in place. "*Go, go, go!*" Manorama shouted, watching the wheels spin, waving his arms, "Keep going!"

But the bus didn't move.

The entire state of Florida is level except for the slight hill that was in front of our bus. We couldn't back up because there was a pine tree behind us. Trying to keep his temple clothes clean, Manorama dug sand out from in front of the wheels.

"Try it again."

The wheels sank deeper. Manorama called the boys'

bus. "We need you to come back and tow us out of the sand."

A local pointed with his cigarette. "Sugar sand. That's the worst."

Others flicked their cigarettes and nodded.

"Only thing worse than sugar sand is gumbo."

There were strong opinions on either side of that one, but everyone had a sugar sand story.

The park's picnic tables filled with people in swimsuits and towels to watch. Kids motored up on their four-wheelers and perspired under the shade trees. They cheered when the boys' bus arrived and PJ tooted the air horn.

Manorama hooked a tow strap to the bus. We were all in uniform—in our Krishna clothes—ready for the show at the temple. Manorama's hands were black from working under the bus.

He shouted, "Go ahead, pull forward, easy, e-e-easy, OK, *stop!*"

"He knows what he's doing," I told the audience. "I've traveled with him across Mexico, off-roading in that same bus."

Both buses roared and sank into the sand as the tow strap tightened. Locals cheered when the silver bus lifted out of its hole and rolled forward.

"He got it."

"I told you he would."

"Don't stop! Don't stop!" Manorama moved his hands in a big circle. "Keep going, keep going!"

I jumped on the bus. My friends waved goodbye

The final performance

from the picnic tables, and the race to the temple was on. Manorama radioed the boys' bus, "Tell Radha Vinod to be ready to MC. He'll have to talk while they set up sound. Don't bother putting on makeup for the drama— it will just melt in this heat."

൜൜൜൜

Alachua, Florida, to Boone, North Carolina

Driving to North Carolina took nine hours. I was alone with my thoughts, with no keeper-upper to entertain me. I'd been surrounded by youth and fun – part of something large, but now I was tiny and vulnerable again, my car squeezing between trucks on the interstate. I passed the turnoff to our old house on Krishna Road and drove on to Boone, my small car straining to climb the hill.

With no other Hare Krishna families living in Boone, we would be alone there, helping Narayan survive his first year of college. If enough people showed interest, though, we might stay and develop a new bhakti community

– every college town should have one. Creating such a community could be an even bigger adventure than the bus tour had been.

The road narrowed and steepened as I approached the Art of Living Ashram at the top of Heavenly Mountain. I parked and gathered my things. The silence of the woods contrasted with the noise of the past several weeks; now, the only sound I could hear was the clicking and gurgling of my car as it cooled. I walked through the breezeway of the condo and paused to take in the view. Our place was on the highest ridgetop, with dozens of mountain ranges fading into the distance. Every condo in the building faced the sunrise. Our room was at the end of the wooden deck, and I knocked on the glass door that led into my new home. Maharha, wiping her hands on her apron, received me warmly as the sky reddened and the shadows grew long.

"I know you'll like it here," she said. "The people are really nice. How was the bus tour?"

Then Narayan appeared at the door carrying textbooks. "Hey, Dad."